The
Believer's
Experience

The Believer's Experience

Maintaining the Scriptural Balance
Between Experience and Truth

ERROLL HULSE

ZONDERVAN
PUBLISHING HOUSE
OF THE ZONDERVAN CORPORATION
GRAND RAPIDS, MICHIGAN 49506

THE BELIEVER'S EXPERIENCE
© 1978 Carey Publications Limited
All rights reserved.

Published by special arrangement with Carey Publications, 5 Fairford Close, Haywards Heath, Sussex, England.

Zondervan edition   1980

Library of Congress Cataloging in Publication Data

Hulse, Erroll, 1931–
    The believer's experience.

    1.   Christian life—1960–   2.   Experience
(Religion)   3.   Pentecostalism.   I.   Title.
BV4501.2.H823   248'.2   79-22304
ISBN 0-310-41701-5

Printed in the United States of America

Contents

Foreword

Rarely has the Church been favoured with such a rich array of helpful books. Expository and biographical volumes come from the printing presses at a rapid rate. As never before we are able to study the lives and experiences of Christians of former times. As we benefit from edifying reading of this character, the question arises in our minds, Where is the power today? Does our experience of the Gospel ring with the same quality as was the case with these worthies of past ages? And whatever has happened to revival? Where today is the conviction of sin and where is the preaching likely to produce it?

Sensing the natural inclination in us all to be content with a head knowledge of spiritual realities, I began to write a series of articles on spiritual experience for the bi-monthly magazine, *Reformation Today*, of which I am the editor. A start was made on the basic subject of humiliation in our experience because of sin. Until there is a sense of need and some humbling there can be no advance, because 'the fear of God is the beginning of wisdom'. That first article has given way to several chapters to do with the moral law. The first article was followed by expositions on joy, love, assurance, patience in tribulation, the baptism of the Spirit and communion with Christ. The original article on love has been completely rewritten and appears now under the title, 'God's love experienced in adoption'.

In writing the book, *An Introduction to the Baptists*, there were many volumes to read. What a contrast with the research and reading required for this book, *The Believer's Experience*!

In writing some chapters I felt like a lonely pioneer. Especially was this the case with the subject of the free grace experience. But it was also true, though to a lesser degree, for the chapters dealing with conversion. I found that the eighteenth century Methodists did justice to that subject. It would have been possible to quote more from their testimonies but I have tried to cover a broad range of examples including contemporary ones such as the moving account related on page 59.

There is no doubt in my mind that experience has been neglected. I am not in the least surprised, therefore, by the advent of the Charismatic movement. If justice is not done to this subject we can be sure that something will come along to fill the vacuum. The perils of swinging from one extreme to another are discussed in the first chapter and in chapter four we study the present scene in earnest.

Some important aspects of experience have been omitted or only briefly mentioned. I would have liked to develop the subject of prayer. For instance Isaiah speaks of mounting up with wings as eagles (Isa. 40:31); and what about Jacob wrestling all night at Peniel? But a halt has to be called somewhere! The Psalms is a handbook in itself on the subject of spiritual experience. I know of three Puritans who wrote books on Psalm 42 which describes the experience of depression. And what (apart from Jeremiah's Lamentations) could match the desolation described in Psalm 88? Material is available on the theme of depression and my friend Herbert Carson is at work on a treatise on the subject of suffering. These factors have disposed me to limit the number of pages devoted to the experience of affliction.

I am indebted to all members of my family and local church for help received, but especially to my wife Lyn and to the cheerful band of helpers who type and proof read. I am grateful too to the Evangelical Library, 78a Chiltern Street, London. The workers there are always willing to extract rare volumes from nooks and crannies and even risk their lives in ascending high ladders in order to bring down the treasures!

Unless otherwise stated the Scripture references are from the King James Version and the example followed of that rendering of the sacred text of using lower case typography for deity. My view is that we are to worship God in the ways he has prescribed and not with inventions of our own, but I respect those whose taste in typography is otherwise.

If this book serves to awaken some to the necessity of valid spiritual experience and helps others to a deeper and broader experience of the love of God in Christ, I shall be encouraged.

November, 1977   Erroll Hulse.

Chapter 1

Why 'The Believer's Experience'?

W̲HEN we speak of spiritual experience, we are referring simply to the whole range of feelings, emotions, affections and resolutions which arise from the heart.

There is little profit to be gained from entering into metaphysical definitions of what is meant by experience. A look at some of the main aspects of experience can provide a better definition of what is meant by that term than trying to fathom the matter from a philosophical point of view.

While it is useful to divide up man for the purpose of studying how he functions we must always remember that he is essentially one – a unity. If we must have division, then most obviously man is body and soul. Man is bipartite – two parts! Then shall the dust return to the earth as it was and the spirit shall return to God who gave it (Eccles. 12:7). When we consider his soul, we may say that understanding is there together with affections and the will. We may then go further and observe that there is a memory and conscience. But a person acts as a unity and seldom does a person stop to say 'Ah! that is my affection' or 'That is my conscience' or 'That is my will'.

Jonathan Edwards points out that what is often called the will or inclination is frequently referred to as the heart! 'Ye have obeyed from the heart,' declares the apostle, 'that form of doctrine which was delivered you' (Rom. 6:17). I prefer the use of the term 'heart' to 'will', and observe that everywhere the idea of heart is associated with experience. It is important, however, that we do not divide the will and heart for reasons other than study. The will moves as it is directed by the affections or heart. What a man likes – that he strives to do. The will is governed by the affections.

Sinners do not love God and therefore what our Lord said to the
Jews of his day 'You will not come to me that you might have life'
(Jn. 5:40) is true of them.   He loves the salvation of sinners and his
invitations go out to all.   He is willing to receive them but they
are not willing to come.   Their hearts (affections) have been stolen
by Satan.   Their hard, world-loving, sin-loving hearts will need to
be exchanged for new, God-loving hearts.

The affections then precede the will, mobilise the will and control
the will.   Man's will is not free as so many imagine.   Man's
will is enchained and dominated by his affections.   The fallen
heart of mankind is deceitful above all things and desperately wicked
(Jer. 17:9).   We can understand then, why it is that fallen men do
not turn to Christ.

Certainly, we must say that the whole of religion can be summed
up by Paul's statement 'love is the fulfilling of the law' (Rom. 13:10).
This 'law' or ten commandments is summed up by one sentence,
'thou shalt love the Lord thy God with all thine heart.'   If that is
done, then the whole will of God will be performed.   The wonder
of the new birth is that the new heart has the moral law inscribed
upon it.   The natural man cannot be subject to God's law, but the
new man delights in it.   He loves or is inclined toward both God
and his law.   His life then is a protracted spiritual experience.

In a sentence I would say that by experience I mean every feeling
that has to do with the heart; humiliation, joy, love, patience, communion.

The first objective of this book is to open up the subject of experience and to demonstrate its essential place in the Christian life.
There are other aims too, such as the need to combat supersainthood,
and to discourage polarisation.

Supersainthood

Many, perhaps most pastors have had to contend at some time or
other with the problem of supersainthood.   This can come in the
form of an arrogant intellectualism displayed by those who believe
they have the last word on doctrine.   Everything is tested for
orthodoxy by the odd one who feels himself to have attained a high

plateau of discernment.   Such individuals can become a menace to a church when they begin to censure everything which they deem to be below the level of the supersainthood they feel themselves to have achieved.   This type however forms a small minority compared to those who have attained the supersainthood of charismatic experience.   From time to time we hear of churches being taken over by this new order of experimental supersainthood.   The second class citizens who are made to feel lukewarm beside the holy heat generated by the super saints, gradually move out of these churches to find spiritual homes elsewhere.

Surely the best possible way to deal with this sort of thing is by showing the great breadth of experience in the Christian life.   In so doing narrow-mindedness or shallowness of all kinds of experimental supersainthood will be exposed.   Spiritual experience is much broader than power experiences alone or joy experiences alone.   Those who have never experienced anything dramatic in that way may in fact be much further advanced in spiritual maturity than those who claim to have had mighty experiences.   Moreover, when we look at the stature of some who have been subject mainly to tribulation experiences, we see that if there must be a comparison they are more likely to be the maxi-saints and the others the mini-saints!

There are too many negative books against pentecostalism.   It is not good enough to respond to books on the baptism of the Spirit with treatises on how to be sure to avoid such a thing.   We need to be positive and we need to look at the subject of experience as a whole.   Spiritual experience is something we simply cannot afford to neglect.   The Ephesian church was reminded of this by the Lord (Rev. 2:4,5).   Their orthodoxy and practice of good works was beyond reproach.   Their experience had declined.   The devotional life of the Christian is just as important as what he believes and what he practises.

Yet another motive for writing on this subject of spiritual experience is the urgent need to avoid extreme reactions.

Polarisation

The charismatic supersainthood movement of today often results in polarisation. One kind of experience is promoted and its expression in an extreme form tends to drive those opposed to it to feel an antagonism to the whole subject. They are 'turned off' to experience as a whole. That is dangerous because experience forms an essential part of Christianity. The Christian life is *experience*. It is loving God with all the heart, mind, soul and body. Anything at all that detracts from that is dangerous. The devil is the genius in the field of polarisation. He is always promoting extremes. When old doctrines are rediscovered, the adversary will be on the lookout to find who can be driven to an extreme to become eccentric or neurotic about doctrine, with the result that others who would benefit much by hard study of excellent books are put off by bad example.

We need too to guard in particular against a polarity developing between mind and emotion. Anti-intellectualism is totally unscriptural. It is by the renewing of the mind that we are conformed to be like Christ (Rom. 12:1,2). But a joyless, emotionless preoccupation with the intellect only, is also contrary to the spiritual life described in the New Testament. If such preoccupation is allied to hyper-orthodoxy and the habit fostered of censuring everything deemed less than orthodox, the effect in a local church can be extremely stultifying and deadening.

The polarisation of intellect and emotion is illustrated by the fact that hyper-orthodoxy is the chief hindrance to growth in some churches. In others perhaps not far removed geographically, confusion and disorder mar the life of the assembly. In the latter it would be surprising to see a single theological book of any significance, whereas in the former, if anyone were to utter a shout of acclamation of joy or praise it would earn many a 'tut-tut' and be regarded as shocking and unseemly.

The same sort of thing can happen with individual subjects. We have the polarisation of Ecumenism on the one hand and Exclusive Brethrenism on the other. Ecumenism spells the demise of true Christianity because it ends up with total confusion in which no longer does anyone have any clear idea of what a Christian is. On the other hand Exclusivism can become every bit as ugly as Pharisaism was when at its ugliest in the apostolic era.

These are days when we must be steadfast and immovable,

grounded and settled in the truth; loving and kind on the one hand, uncompromisingly firm on the other. We must not allow ourselves to be pushed around in our beliefs because of the failure of others to maintain balanced, scriptural Christianity.

NOTES

Francis A. Schaeffer in his little book *The New Super-Spirituality* describes a variety of supersaints including those who think they have the final word on prophecy. He even refers to a type of supersaint three decades ago when some ministers in Holland were recognised by their striped trousers and their bicycles which were about two inches higher than others! But Schaeffer is firm in the absolute sense with 'super-spiritual ones who are determined to bring everyone else into their own kind of bondage'. 'As much as we love you, and you know how much we love you, we regretfully say you have to leave.'

Chapter 2

How Experience came to be Emphasised

THE revolution we have lived to see is wide in its ramifications. America and Britain emerged from the Second World War battered and weary. The Cold War and the Korean war had to be fought and the peoples soldiered on with a fair degree of unity. It was in the 1960s that the rising generation began to question and repudiate a way of life that for centuries had been accepted as the norm. Protests and riots hit the cities of America. The drug traffic problem, hitherto confined to ghettos, began to spread in epidemic proportions throughout schools in the country.[1] The trend begun then continues today. Few areas are without some broken-hearted parents. Perplexed Moms and Dads simply could not understand why their offspring should behave like morons when they had been given everything. Why should the respectable lives of affluent people be disgraced by the non-ambitious, rebellious and drop-out mentality and practice of the new generation? The truth was that the easy-going materialism combined with an empty, powerless, nominal kind of Christianity offered no appeal, no dynamic and no reality to the young. Frustrated and bored, they expressed their rejection in vehement and sometimes violent terms.

Reference to happenings in London can give a clue to a few contributory factors. The London School of Economics had sought solutions to problems in the area of economics and philosophy without success. When the Maharishi arrived in the 1960s, he was welcomed by the LSE. Before packed audiences at the Albert Hall he demonstrated how to find experience within oneself. By following his instructions and sayings – mm, mm, mm, mm – one could take a trip within. Such an exercise lasting only twenty minutes could make all the difference! One could work harder, concentrate better and, when insulted, resist retaliatory feelings.

The Beatles were numbered among his disciples. Their music became an enormous factor in conveying the message of experience by 'trips', whether 'trips' within or 'trips' without. Psychedelic music was the 'in' thing. The stress was on experience.

Luther said that, after theology, music was the most powerful influence in the world. For good or ill, that point has been illustrated at different times. The Beatles had a tremendous influence in loosening a whole generation from old ways and traditions. The spirit of their music made it much easier to break free from traditions and question old values. In search of dynamism the new generation began to question and reject moral values. This led to the sex revolution. 'Why shouldn't we?' has always been a question, although family tradition and fear of the dangers involved in promiscuity form a powerful restraint. The most important consideration of all is God's moral law. God's ten commandments are absolute and binding. He will judge and punish every transgressor. But the power of humanistic and secular thought has all but blotted out the old values and blunted former sensitivities, thus making way for the sex revolution.

With the demise of Christianity as a potent force in society the most powerful restraint was gone. Contraception minimised physical dangers. This left the influence of parents. In many cases an unhappy home scene and a poor example did little to inspire loyalty to the family. But the main issue was the vacuum left by a form of religion which was destitute of power. This is not to say that all practising, orthodox, Bible-believing families have been unscathed by the revolution of recent years. History furnishes adequate examples of those who have 'prodigalised' from the best homes. Judas 'apostatised' from the best circle of intimate fellowship that ever existed. Nevertheless, it must be observed that a home life which lacks love, wisdom and flexibility, and which is too rigid or too legalistic, can be self-defeating. However, by far the greatest proportion of casualties in the drug and sex revolution have come from the affluent, well-to-do middle class strata where nominal Christianity has been despised and rejected for the worthless and futile thing that it is.

Behind the drug revolution and the sex revolution lies the driving desire for 'kicks', for experience. Behind the revolution in philosophy, which has been going on for centuries, lies the desire for answers. The revolution in philosophy has prepared the way and made fertile ground for the drug and sex revolution. The cultural change we have seen is the outward manifestation of the revolution going

on in society.   Modern art and modern music give expression to and
illustrate the various facets of that revolution.

A notable feature in all this is that the revolution as an intellectual
force is confined to a small elite.   With the rest it is experiential
rather than intellectual.   For instance, if you ask an average devotee
of the new life-style to tell you about Martin Heidegger's distinction
between 'authentic' and 'unauthentic' existence, it is unlikely that
he will even know about it.   But the philosophy has filtered through
the mass media, and the concept that we should break away from
every convention and discipline and every kind of life-style that
might threaten our own personal authentication is rife.   Similarly,
if you ask about the influence of Sartre you will find little if any
knowledge about Jean-Paul Sartre or his philosophy.   Yet at the
same time the philosophy of self-assertion and self-authentication
without reference to any moral absolutes is being lived out by the
new generation which is generally sympathetic towards the whole
idea of finding reality in experience.   A new-generation person may
himself not be a drug-addict and may never have read anything by
Soren Kierkegaard, but more likely than not he will respond to
ideas of experience whether presented by Eastern religion, by Yoga
or by Transcendental Meditation.

The experiential character of this revolution can be seen in the
protests, the riots and the destruction that has come in the wake of
the movement.   Old values and institutions have been torn down,
but there is little of a constructive or inspired nature to replace what
is removed.   The emphasis is not on the intellect, or on thinking
out positive and practical solutions, but rather on the assertion of
feelings and on the release of tensions.

We see then, that since the 1960s in particular, the stress has been
on the search for experience.   The stress has not been on doctrine
and truth as the basis for experience.   Indeed, doctrine has been
regarded as the enemy of experience.   Unhappily (and sometimes
with justification) preaching and doctrine have been viewed as
dry, academic and irrelevant, things which are likely to destroy real
feeling, discourage emotion and paralyse freedom.   The cry has
gone up, 'I want to feel, I want to know [that is experience], I want
to *be* [that is authenticate myself].'

The general atmosphere in the world today is of such a kind as
to bring about ideal conditions for the birth and increase of the
Charismatic Movement which has penetrated all the major denominations.

Especially is this true of the Roman Catholic Church.   The people have become tired of being spectators of an oft-repeated ritual. There has been a call for participation and for experience. During the debates of Vatican II, 1963, Cardinal Suenens opposed Cardinal Ruffini because he wished to restrict charismatic gifts to the clergy. By way of conclusion Cardinal Suenens made a fascinating statement, 'Without the shepherds the Church would be undisciplined; but without the charisma, it would be sterile. Therefore the pastors must heed the warnings of St. Paul and take care not to "stifle the Spirit".' Michael Harper in his book *Let My People Grow*[2] comments, 'if ever a door was opened this was it'. During 1967 the Catholic charismatic renewal began in universities in Indiana and Pennsylvania. Subsequently the experience-centred Charismatic Movement invaded and established itself not only in Roman Catholicism but in most of the major denominations.

Michael Green points out that after more than sixty years the Ecumenical Movement 'is showing some signs of effeteness'.[3] Effeteness is an appropriate word. It means (from fetus), no longer fertile, worn out with age or marked by weakness and decadence. Michael Green is astute in his observation. In contrast with the infertility of the Ecumenical Movement the Charismatic Movement has proliferated with ideas and vitality. We should not be surprised at the growth it has shown.

The increase of the movement is seen in the bookshops many of which are completely dominated by preference for Charismatic books. Some time ago I went into a Roman Catholic bookshop in London to buy everything I could on the subject. My enquiry was not only warmly welcomed and attended to by fervent enthusiasm, but I was also zealously invited to an interdenominational Charismatic meeting, being given all the details. Michael Green in speaking of unity observes that 'the charismatics show a degree of love and commitment to one another which is probably unrivalled in any other strand of contemporary Christianity'. He qualifies the statement by pointing out that 'it is sometimes restricted to the like-minded, those Christians who have had a similar experience of the Spirit'.[4] Let us go on to examine the question of success.

---

[1] In surveying the past I acknowledge help received from a tape-cassette exposition by George E. Gardiner whose booklet *The Corinthian Catastrophe* (Kregel) has also been useful.

[2] p. 96.

[3] *I believe in the Holy Spirit*, p. 207.

[4] ibid.

Chapter 3

How can we explain the success of the Charismatic Movement?

AT the outset clarification is needed with regard to what is meant by Charismatic, and what by success.   Self-examination will follow.

The Charismatic movement varies in character from region to region.   In some areas it is fizzling out.   In others it is gaining momentum.   Some of the large gatherings are carefully controlled, the more ecstatic elements being muted or played down.   The leaders are anxious to be recognised as part of the evangelical body. In this way confidence can be won and greater gains made.   Like the Church of Rome all kinds of practices and doctrines can be accommodated.   In that sense the Charismatic movement is counterfeit.   We should heed the warnings of experienced ministers who have had to counsel and help those injured by the movement. In some places a fearful spiritual wreckage has been left behind. Compromise should be avoided.

We must recognize that the exuberant, uninhibited approach in the meetings with thrilling singing accompanied by tambourines and orchestra is a potent factor.   The emphasis is on love.   The critical faculties of analysis tend to be dulled by the aura of it all, if not, for the vast majority, forgotten altogether!   Although not spoken in as many words the message is implied in the most cogent way that this is 'it' !   This is the revival of the latter days!   This is the millennial glory!

The movement is different and changes all the time, but here in Sussex I have observed a psychic element similar to that witnessed in Africa in mass gatherings of the Zionist sects.   There is the same emphasis on rhythm and excitement.   If the meetings here were not muted dancing would break out.   The dancing element is much more uninhibited among the Africans, a reminder that culture and tradition have to be reckoned with.

Many are mightily impressed.   Some find genuine release for feelings long repressed by legalistic religion or other frustrating influences.   It does not help to 'bash' the whole thing because complex factors such as background, personality and taste enter into it.   Women often predominate.

We must now consider the question of success.   The Scripture declares that only those who keep the rules will gain the crown.   If the groundsmen change the length of the athletic stadium from 400 metres to 340 metres then you can put me down for a world record for both 400 and 800 metres.   In a year's time, however, I may have a nervous breakdown because of all the unpleasant implications and difficulties arising out of a counterfeit situation.

Between thirty and forty evangelical ministers in this county of Sussex complain that the Charismatics have no scruples in carrying off of sheep and lambs to their house groups or house churches.   As ministers of varying denominations we have a very high regard for each other and for church discipline.   When important principles are broken then we question very much the use of the word 'success'.

Having said that, however, we realize that our churches and worship services are open to criticism.   Compared with the mass meeting in which there are no restraints the worship service of a church can be (but need not be) a dull affair.   Sometimes cults like Jehovah Witnesses and Mormons can be a reproof by way of pointing to the zeal that we ought to have.   In a different way the Charismatic movement as an extreme and reactionary phenomenon can point to the improvements which can be made in our worship services.

Let me illustrate this by referring to the delicate matter of our relationship to the Holy Spirit.

The Holy Spirit is a person and besides thinking of him as the eternal God possessing all the attributes of Deity we should think of him simply as a person.   To stress the point of 'personhood' let me put it this way.   Suppose a person by the name of Mr. Omnipotent became a member of our local church.   (With respect we shall call him Mr. O. simply to stress the personal aspect.)   Mr. O. possesses a unique power to draw and convert people of all kinds. The first Sunday Mr. O. telephones the Pastor and requests that instead of our usual hymns and tunes we should sing psalms in modern renderings to modern music.   The Pastor replies that he would dearly like to do that, especially since the renderings are accurate and the music respectable and refreshing. But Mr. O's request is politely turned down on the grounds that certain people in the church will be offended, and interpret such a thing as retrogression into Arminianism. Their view is that since Mr. O. is omnipotent there is no need for anything extravagant or different.

During the day Mr. O. phones again. This time he requests that a modern version of the Bible be used for the readings in the evening service. The Chinese, Indian and Black immigrants and other visitors from abroad will understand it much more readily. Again Mr. O's request is kindly but firmly refused on the grounds that some will be offended. Surely if Mr. O. is omnipotent such measures which might offend some are not needed. After all if the sermon was preached in Hungarian and went on for an agonizing hour he could still convert people because of his sovereign power!

Over a period of time several other requests are made by Mr. O. The old Victorian structure is cold and forbidding. Most of the members live in modern, attractive houses but the church is nothing like that. In its decor it is well below the standard of the homes. The answer is always the same! Surely if Mr. O. is omnipotent he does not require so ludicrous a thing as modern architecture, comfortable seats and healthy ventilation. Surely such things directly contradict Mr. O's omnipotence. The more difficult conditions are, the more credit Mr. O. will receive when people are converted. Staggeringly, in answer to the fervent prayers and hard work by some in the church Mr. O. does save a handful. Despite tremendous personal discouragements, the pastor is sustained by observing that Mr. O. has not departed in disgust because his requests have had to be turned down.

However, one day something happens (which the pastor knew all along would happen) which comes as a terrific shock to the church. They hear that Mr. O. has been regularly attending another church in the locality. The appalling situation is that that particular church attended by Mr. O. is unorthodox and Ecumenically inclined. Mr. O. has not only taken large numbers to that church but some have been converted there. A few simply refuse to accept these facts and say that it will all come to nothing. But it does not. Such incredulity is shown to be unworthy because some of the very people converted in the unorthodox church down the road, where Mr. O. has been doing so well, have become Reformed, are no longer Charismatic and actually see the Ecumenical movement as a hoax! One or two of the converts have even become

Reformed Baptist pastors! There is no question therefore about the fact that despite their faults Mr. O. has favoured the unorthodox church in an amazing way!

Not wishing to be disrespectful to Mr. O., some of the very orthodox feel the whole thing to be rather disgusting and very disheartening to say the least, so they ask their pastor to interview Mr. O. and find out how it is that he can be so inconsistent as to ignore the fact that they are *the* people who hold 'the truth' – and yet he appears to have blessed those others so much more?

Mr. O. is interviewed and this is what he says: 'Well, you see, I asked you to make several changes, all of which were entirely consistent with the Bible. These you refused because you were afraid of offending the traditional element in your Church. You will see from the Scriptures and history that I always draw and convert God's elect but that I use natural means, such as warm friendship and the communication of truth in a comprehensible way. I enjoy my work and since you made it cold for me and would not do as I suggested I decided that it would be more congenial for everyone concerned for the people to be saved through the other church where they would be more sympathetically received and their needs better catered for. You know that without exception I maintain the right to work where I please. In this case your disobedience is more offensive to me than the blindness and errors which are so obvious in the other church. In any case I am well able to convert those in my own time. Knowing the end from the beginning I always accomplish all to the praise of God's glory. Though this may not seem to be the case to you now, it will be so in the end. And now, how about reconsidering those requests I made in the first place, and how about making more room for me, a person, in your church?'

We have compared an ordinary orthodox Evangelical church with a lively unorthodox church, but what about the thousands of churches which have died, churches which have Ichabod written over them! The glory has departed. Here in Sussex we are literally surrounded by dying or already dead hyper-Calvinistic churches and churches which have died or are dying because of Modernism (which simply means a rejection of the Bible as God's inspired word). When the Holy Spirit has departed the disastrous results can be seen by the lack of faith and vital experience. How sad the plight of these churches that are without experience and whose members and services resemble the scene portrayed in Coleridge's *Ancient Mariner*.

They groaned, they stirred, they all uprose,
Nor spake, nor moved their eyes,
It had been strange, even in a dream
To have seen those dead men, rise.

The helmsman steered, the ship moved on,
Yet never a breeze up-blew,
The Mariners all 'gan work the ropes,
Where they were wont to do,
They raised their limbs like lifeless tools—
We were a ghastly crew.

How long will young people endure such a situation? Not long! What faith is to be seen, or expectancy, in dead churches? There is expectancy with the Charismatics. They are expecting direct messages and revelations. We may not agree with all that but let us ask what we are expecting? What faith are we exercising? Are we expecting new people to arrive in response to our invitations? Are we striving for and believing God for a bigger missionary budget? Are we vital and earnest and exercising faith in church planting? If we have to say 'no' to all these things then it should not surprise us in the least that the Charismatics seem to be multiplying and increasing in their influence. We need to be crystal clear about the reasons why.

The crippling traditionalism and consequent deadness of some orthodox churches has been explained and the consequent attractiveness of the Charismatic Movement adverted to. This attractiveness is often external. A closer examination reveals that it is superficial. In our reaction against the cold cynicism of lifeless orthodoxy, and attraction to that which is uninhibited and joyful, we can too easily overlook the stern realities and rigorous demands of the Gospel. We are influenced far more than we realize by the age in which we live. There is also a concern that we should be seen as the happiest people on earth rather than the holiest. Who would deny that we all tend to turn to a chapter on the experience of joy more readily than to one on tribulation and suffering? The natural appetite tends to go in the direction of thrills and spills, stories and anecdotes, excitements and sensations.

The Christian life is enormously exacting and should be filled with thoughtful study, persevering prayer, spiritual discipline, practical living and an earnest application of the principles of righteousness to our thoughts, words and deeds.

Balanced expository preaching is calculated to meet the need and fill the spiritual vacuum of our day. If the vacuum is not filled with the truth expounded and applied in its fullness, that vacuum will be filled with something else. There may be a lusting for novelties and entertainments but there is also in many a genuine desire for spiritual reality. This vacuum will be filled! If it is not filled with living by the Word of God it will be by the wonders and amazements of those who offer a variety of inspirations. The Charismatic Movement is moving in everywhere where a vacuum, due to the lack of expository preaching and balanced church life, has been left. Pew filling alone will never satisfy. I know personally a very gifted couple of unusual personality and charm who for years attended a famous preaching house. Eventually they reacted against being hearers only without any guidance as to church integration and service. 'Body care' became a lively issue for them. They whole-heartedly entered into Pentecostalism by way of a house group. I do not doubt that they had the most profitable experience and reviving in their hearts. Needs were met which had not been met before. After a few years the house group broke up and this couple joined a local church. The basic requirement of expository preaching turned out to be essential after all, but this time they joined a church where there was fellowship to go with it.

When Christians 'go Charismatic' it is not the end of the story. If it is through disillusionment or dissatisfaction let us examine ourselves. Is there a lack of reality in our preaching or in our lives?

Chapter **4**

The Blessings, Main Problem and Dangers of the Charismatic Experience

1. The blessings

DO you know what it is for the Holy Spirit to fall upon you? Do you know what it is to be taken hold of by the Spirit? In the history of the Church such experiences are not confined to those of Pentecostal persuasion. But the Pentecostal denominations and modern neo-Pentecostal Movement has majored upon power experiences. The word 'neo-Pentecostal' has been overshadowed by the term 'Charismatic'. This has strengthened the Charismatic Movement, as the word 'Charismatic' conjures up all kinds of ideas and attracts many. The difference between Pentecostals and Charismatics ought to be noted. Many Pentecostal pastors and leaders disown the Charismatic Movement because it is experience-centred in the sense that experience, rather than clearly defined doctrine, is used by the Charismatics as a basis of unity. Much therefore of what is to be stated later in this chapter does not apply to Pentecostals who are determined to base their practice on the Bible. There are a few Pentecostals who are Reformed in their doctrine of salvation and with such men we have much in common. We share with them the sorrow of observing the confusion which results when truth is neglected as the standard by which all our claims and practices must be tested.

What Pentecostals and Charismatics have in common is their stress on the baptism of the Spirit as a second experience, speaking in tongues, and the belief that all the gifts of the Spirit such as prophecies, healing and miracles should be in operation throughout this age until Christ comes.

It would be foolish to deny that there are blessings in these Charismatic experiences. He who would deny that shows that he has not been truly involved himself by way of experience. Joy, zeal, love, devotion and evangelistic fervour flow out of a genuine experience of the Spirit. At an early stage of my Christian life I was sustained and strengthened by Pentecostalism. It was a way of life. I had not been introduced to free grace teaching and was very weak in my grasp of Christian doctrine. In my search for reality I found Pentecostalism to be alive and powerful. For me it completely overshadowed the Keswick movement which I also tried as a possible answer in looking for dynamic and authentic Christian experience. The devotional addresses, unity and fellowship at Keswick were heartwarming, but for me the week ended in depression. The time was supposed to end in a climax of blessing but it turned out to be an anti-climax. There was no crescendo and no Pentecost to fill the vacuum created by my sincere and full-surrender. I let go and let God and all that happened was that I landed up in the same old world where I was before. The Keswick Convention situation may have improved in recent years but there has been a lack of definitive doctrine in the devotional addresses of Keswick and certainly little offered in the area of experience which could match the excitement of Pentecostalism.

It would be wrong to allow disagreement or prejudice to cloud our judgment about Pentecostals. Many of them maintain a better Christian life and testimony than orthodox anti-Pentecostals. That does not endorse their teaching and nor does it condemn orthodox belief. To attain a happy balance of truth, experience and practice is not easy. Many of our blessings are mixed. For me at that period Pentecostalism was a blessing but it was a mixed blessing and in the course of time it could not stand up to the tests set it by the teaching of Scripture. Gradually a transformation took place. It can be simply expressed as follows:

1. $\dfrac{\text{Experience}}{\text{Doctrine}}$ 2. $\dfrac{\text{Doctrine}}{\text{Experience}}$

In another chapter I describe the free grace experience for which

I shall never cease to thank God and which I have never doubted to be the foundational or authentic experience which has vindicated and confirmed Christianity for me and grounded and settled me once and for all in the conviction that 'this is the real thing!'   I welcome spiritual experiences but I need nothing else to confirm the Gospel to me as *the* truth beyond the free grace so beautifully summed up in Galatians 2:20.

At this point it would be appropriate to quote the blessings of Pentecostalism as expressed by someone wholly persuaded of the rightness of that position and currently involved in it.   J. Rodman Williams writing in *Christianity Today*[1] sums up the blessings of the Charismatic Movement as one who has been committed to it for ten years.   He outlines the elements as follows:

1. the recovery of a vital and dynamic sense of the reality of the Christian faith
2. a striking renewal of the community of believers as a fellowship (koinonia) of the Holy Spirit
3. the manifestation of a wide range of 'spiritual gifts', with parallels drawn from 1 Corinthians 12-14
4. the experience of 'baptism in the Holy Spirit', often accompanied by 'tongues', as a radical spiritual renewal
5. the re-emergence of a spiritual unity that essentially transcends denominational barriers
6. the rediscovery of a dynamic for bearing comprehensive witness to the Good News of Jesus Christ
7. the revitalization of the eschatological perspective

Points 1, 2, 5, and 6 are by no means unique to the Charismatic Movement.   Point 7 is not clear inasmuch as the eschatological perspective as it pertains to America is probably dispensationalism and few subjects have divided Christians and marred their unity and relationships more than that!

That expository preaching is not in the list is noteworthy and no reference is made to reformation of the churches and practical Christian living.

Points 3 and 4 are Pentecostal distinctives which we will discuss presently as the central problem.

Thomas A. Smail in his book *Reflected Glory* gives his personal testimony.   He declares the blessing of the Charismatic experience in these terms:

a releasing discovery of the limitless life and power that God sought to make available to me, of the largely unappropriated reality of praise and prayer, of a new sense of being personally addressed by the word of God in the Scripture, a new pastoral empathy with people and a new ability to diagnose and deal with their needs, a new confidence and reality in preaching and worship, and a new sense of victory at some outstanding points of defeat in the moral struggle—all leading to a new confidence of hope in what God was going to do in my own life and in the life of his Church.[2]

I would not dispute or disparage any point of this testimony but only make the comment that all that is described has happened to others who have had no knowledge of Pentecostalism. Let me cite just one example. Christmas Evans after fifteen years of spiritual barrenness was delivered in an experience which he describes like this:

On a day ever to be remembered by me, as I was going from Dolgellau to Machynlleth, climbing up towards Cader Idris, I considered it to be incumbent upon me to pray, however hard I felt in my heart and however worldly the frame of my spirit was. Having begun in the name of Jesus, I soon felt as it were, the fetters loosening, and the old hardness of heart softening, and, as I thought, mountains of frost and snow dissolving and melting within me. This engendered confidence in my soul in the promise of the Holy Ghost. I felt my whole mind relieved from some great bondage. Tears flowed copiously and I was constrained to cry out for the gracious visits of God, by restoring to my soul the joys of his salvation and to visit the churches in Anglesey that were under my care. I embraced in my supplications all the churches of the saints and nearly all the ministries in the principality by their names. This struggle lasted for three hours. It rose again and again, like one wave after another, on a high, flowing tide driven by a strong wind, till my nature became faint by weeping and crying. I resigned myself to Christ, body and soul, gifts and labours, every hour of every day that remained for me and all my cares I committed to Christ. The road was mountainous and lonely and I was wholly alone and suffered no interruption in my wrestling with God.

After this Christmas Evans made a covenant with God pledging himself to renew devotion to his service. The first indication he received of improvement was a change of attitude in two of his deacons – a new earnestness for prosperity. Large numbers began to be added to the churches again. In the two succeeding years six hundred persons were added.[3]

That there are blessings in the Pentecostal experiences of today I do not dispute. The construction placed upon those experiences and the conclusions which are drawn from them I do question.

2. The main problem

The main problem confronting us is simply, Have the charismatic gifts ceased or not? If they have not ceased and were never meant to cease, then the Charismatics have a cogent case when they say that this explains why the Church is weak. Also there is a strong argument that we should go on strike and concentrate on the regaining of that which has been lost. This is a problem far greater than the questions posed by the second blessing issue. Thomas Smail in his book already referred to rightly concedes that there is ultimately only one blessing:

'How many blessings are there?' The New Testament answer is 'essentially one'. God has given us his one gift of himself in his Son, and everything else is contained in him. 'Blessed be the God and Father of our Lord Jesus Christ, who has blessed us *in Christ with every spiritual blessing* in the heavenly places' (Eph. 1:3). However many and varied our spiritual experiences, they all have their unity and significance in the fact that they all proceed from him, reflect him, and glorify him.[4]

In the chapter on the baptism of the Spirit I point out that when we are united to Christ we are united to the whole of him. Regeneration and conversion together with justification and forgiveness do not form a first blessing with sanctification to follow at a later date as a second blessing. The main problem is not the second blessing issue. No, the main problem is the one that has been asserted and which can be stated in a different way as follows. Is this entire dispensation supposed to be extraordinary and charismatic? Is this whole time from Christ's first advent to his second advent supposed to be filled with the miraculous and extraordinary gifts or not?

This main problem could be settled in a moment if we could find one statement which plainly or conclusively declares that it was God's purpose to withdraw the charismata. No such text can be found. This discovery by no means ends the dispute because the next question to be posed is this: Can it be proved by inference from the Scripture that the Charismatic period ended with the apostles? As theologians might express it, is there a biblical hermeneutic which is decisive? Is there a principle inherent in the Scriptures which decides the issue? I believe there is.

The majority of those in the Evangelical Reformed tradition have been fully persuaded that the inferential argument is perfectly sound, valid and adequate.   Those who have written on the subject include John Owen, Jonathan Edwards, George Smeaton, James Buchanan, B. B. Warfield and in our generation Walter Chantry.

It is alleged that to argue by inference is not to argue biblically. Furthermore it is thought that there is a tendency for Reformed believers to argue in a philosophical or speculative way.   In reply to this I would agree that much care should be taken to avoid the snare of reasoning in an unbiblical fashion.   However in this case I am persuaded that the observations and arguments regarding the cessation of the charismata are not only biblical, but thoroughly biblical!   I believe that it is of the utmost importance that we observe that the Bible shows that God does act in a different way during different epochs.   The most simple mind can observe plain facts of Bible history to which our attention is sometimes drawn. 'John did no miracle' (Jn. 10:41).   There was a time when our Lord appeared by theophany and a time when he did not.   The observations of such matters belongs to the order of biblical theology not philosophy.   And biblical theology is of paramount importance.

My own summary of the inferential position I advance as follows. Apostles were temporary.   All but the smallest of the Charismatic groups (the Apostolic Pentecostals) concede that.   If they were temporary, then already we have established the principle of the extraordinary and temporary as against the ordinary and permanent. There are passages which show that the wonders, signs and miracles were given specifically to attest the veracity of the Gospel as established by the apostles.   After all, the entire revelation depended on them (Heb. 2:4, 2 Cor. 12:12, Eph. 2:20).   Miraculous power was not confined to the apostles.   Stephen, who was not an apostle, obviously possessed the gift of miracles.   This was because it was the apostolic testimony *at that time* that required vindication.   I have never read of any person since the apostolic period who has possessed that same gift to perform perfect miracles as was possessed by Peter and Stephen.   Not for one moment do I deny that God *could* give the gift today but if he gave the gift of miracles it would be to attest something other than what was being attested while the apostles lived.   The mighty miracles, signs and wonders attested that they were telling the truth.   We need no such attestation in that way today because such would be a slur and would cast a shadow over the Word of God.   The Word itself is a perfect vindication of the truth of the Christ even in all its details.   I would regret anybody insisting upon miracles to prove the New Testament record to be true.   It is true without any further miracles or signs.   If a person produced miracles out of God's compassion for sick people we would only rejoice in the mighty power of God and in his mercy, but this is different from rejoicing in a vindication that Jesus is raised from the dead. If someone is still not sure about the resurrection he must give attention to the more sure word of prophecy and not look for further miracles (2 Pet. 1:19). If they hear not Moses and the prophets neither will they be persuaded though one rose from the dead (Luke 16:31).

The gifts of tongues, interpretation of tongues, and prophecies were, according to B. B. Warfield in his chapter on the cessation of the charismata, common to all the churches. Although he was not there to see it we see no reason for rejecting his assertion. According to Edwards in his exposition of 1 Corinthians 13 these oral gifts were a means of edification until that which was perfect was established. Those who reject the possibility of establishing any argument from 1 Corinthians 13 on exegetical grounds should not be too quick to dismiss the principles produced by Edwards on that matter. There is a fundamental difference between ministering to a local church which possesses the whole Bible in writing, and by contrast, a pioneering situation in which the Scriptures have yet to be translated and published in the language of the people concerned. Edwards reasons well and powerfully when he contrasts the imperfect and infantile with the perfect and mature, supporting this further by a comparison of the present state with that which will be perfect in the consummate sense. Those who contemptuously dismiss Edwards with a wave of the hand tell us more about themselves than about Edwards!

Some have pointed out that if we concede that the absence of the Scriptures in writing constitutes an extraordinary situation, we should also concede that in such a case of infant development the situation could be assisted by the impression of extraordinary miracles or signs to attest the truth of the gospel.

My own response to that argument is that it is a sound and reasonable one. I would add that if God does give supernatural signs they will be of such an order that nobody could dispute them, just as nobody could contradict the miracles of Christ and his apostles. There was no strain involved. The power signs just seemed to tumble out of heaven. They were given by God, with the stress on *given*. They were not extracted. History shows that men such as William Carey had to follow a long hard road of toil. Miracles could have tumbled out of heaven, but they did not. Carey could hardly have been blamed for a blockage. It would be absurd to attribute the lack of miracles to a lack of faith. Carey showed faith of superlative quality in persevering through so many difficulties.

The actual purpose of the gifts to attest or to edify provides a basis or principle upon which to distinguish between the extraordinary and the ordinary, the permanent and temporary. The lists of gifts vary. There is more stress on the supernatural gifts in 1 Corinthians 12 because Paul was dealing with the charismata in particular in that letter, whereas only prophecy belongs to the extraordinary category in the gifts mentioned in the Romans 12 passage.

Many of the Protestant consensus, including an increasing number of ex-Pentecostalists like myself, are convinced by the inferential argument outlined above, the main principle of which is well summed up by Warfield as follows:

There is an inseparable connection of miracles with revelation as its mark or credential. Miracles do not appear on the page of Scripture vagrantly here, there and everywhere indifferently without assignable reason. They belong to revelation periods and appear only when God is speaking to his people through accredited messengers. Their abundant display in the Apostolic Church is the mark of the richness of that age in revelation; and when this revelation period closed, the period of miracle-working had passed by also as a matter of course.[5]

My personal belief on this matter is not that God cannot give a prophecy or a miracle. He can do anything he pleases. To believe in the cessation of the Charismata does not mean the cessation of the supernatural. What is meant is that whereas the miraculous was the norm with the apostles, now it is exceptional. We have no need to fret about it or get worked up about it. A miracle after the New Testament pattern is so plain, powerful and irrefutable that it would be futile to argue about it. Probably God has done miracles and given some true prophecies since the apostolic era but they are of an exceptional and temporary category and not permanent.

What about those who are not convinced? Such contend that we who are convinced have had our minds shut whereas theirs are open. Whatever position we hold we are all without exception required to test all things. Such testings have convinced many that if there is to be another Pentecostal age it has not arrived yet. For instance what are we to say of believers like Ken Haarhof who describes his experience in this way:

I spent over 20 years in the Pentecostal atmosphere of the Apostolic Faith Mission, Full Gospel Church and Assemblies of God, of which four years were in full-time ministry. I attended every major campaign in South Africa from the 1950s onward, including those of Branham, Oral Roberts, Lorne Fox and many others of local fame. I acted as usher in healing lines and as a counsellor in enquiry rooms. I lived through climax and anti-climax. I climbed the mountain peaks of expectation. I waded through the valleys of disappointment. I laid hands on the sick. I rebuked death. I prophesied. I spoke in tongues. I interpreted. I would now say, in all sincerity, that I saw and experienced nothing which would lead me to believe that Pentecostalism offers anything along the lines of the New Testament Churches' experience. I am often asked to explain my attitude in retrospect to my Pentecostal experiences, particularly that of tongues. Pentecostals feel that if it is not of God it must necessarily be of Satan, but I have found a more charitable view among their non-Pentecostal Christian fellows. I would say that my experience can be explained in terms of a combination of the following factors. 1. A sincere desire for a deeper experience. 2. A faulty doctrinal basis. 3. Manipulative indoctrination. 4. Enthusiasm. 5. A charged atmosphere. 6. A demonstration or example of how it is done.[6]

The main problem as to whether the charismata have ceased or not is not theoretical only. It is a problem which affects our form of worship and practice in a radical and dramatic way. We should not be surprised therefore that the adversary has found much fertile ground to arouse the most fierce and intense animosities and divisions among Christians.

Those who believe with all their heart that they have had a genuine supernatural experience understandably do not take kindly to those who are quite unconvinced that this is so. When it comes to contention we find that experience is always stronger than an argument. People generally feel intensely about their experiences and resent those who are incredulous or unimpressed by their descriptions. We should note that when we move from doctrine to the pragmatic or experimental we move to ground which is full of uncertainty. I can prove at any time the content of John chapter three, verse three, but how can I prove to anyone with any finality or ultimate certainty that I have had a dream, seen a vision or felt an elation? Observers cannot climb inside me to verify that my experiences are real and not exaggerated or imagined.

What should be our response if the local church to which we belong turns from an orthodox to a Pentecostal basis? If we are not convinced that this is the beginning of the millennium, the ushering in again of that which should have always been present and should never have been lost – how are we to react? So great is the difference and so traumatic is the vexation of being required to believe that which is incredible that I have no hesitation in saying that a transfer (if possible) to another church accompanied with a minimum of ill-feeling constitutes in most cases the wisest action. Secession is always preferable to schism.[7]

Viewed pragmatically, what are the main reasons why many reject Pentecostal claims? Ken Haarhof distinguishes between the vocal gifts and the power gifts such as healing miracles. He points out that the gifts to do with speech greatly 'outproportion' the miracles of power. Almost all lay claim to tongues, fewer to interpretation of tongues, fewer still to prophecy, while those who would be ready to come forward as raisers of the dead hardly exist at all. Does not this disparity or disproportion contrast strongly with the apostolic era?

With regard to the vocal gifts my eyes began to open when I insisted on writing down interpretations of tongues and prophecies and comparing them with Scripture. The contrast in content and the poor quality were such that I could not accept that the vocal messages constituted the inspired work of the Holy Spirit. Also the way in which tongues are induced or taught contrasted completely with the way in which the Spirit fell upon believers in the apostolic period.

In this connection George Gardiner, an ex-Pentecostal minister who spent twenty-two years in the Charismatic Movement, has made some interesting observations about tongues. 'Give me any group of people,' he boldly declares, 'who will do what I say, who will go through the ritual and do it with sincerity, and, in a matter of time, I will have them all speaking in ecstatic speech.'[8] But he does qualify this further by insisting that controls be dropped and inhibitions be removed.

A further problem existed for me which has also perplexed many and that is the nature of the tongues spoken. Having participated myself and having seen and heard others in action I could never agree that these are real languages or in fact any kind of language which has a proper grammatical construction. The more I go on in the Christian life the more fond I become of language study and the more I am impressed by the complexity of languages. I find it hard to believe that angels would use languages that consist of basic sounds repeated over and over again, that is, language without proper syntax. I remain unpersuaded that glossolalia as it is practised today is the language of angels (1 Cor. 13:1). I think they would be quite offended at such a claim. Some Pentecostal friends I have spoken with do not claim that tongues form the speech of angels but the issue is still relevant because it is hard to accept that the Holy Spirit is the inspirer of gibberish or that it is gibberish that is interpreted into the speech of men.

There are several books on tongues which are full of interest and information by men such as Parnell, Gromacki, Hoekema, and John Kildahl. After many years of research and analysis Kildahl came to the following conclusion in answering the question, is tongues a spiritual gift?

We have shown that speaking in tongues can be learned, almost as other abilities are learned. Whether one calls the practice a gift of the Spirit is, then, a matter of individual choice. Speaking in tongues does make the individual feel better, and theologically it is perhaps possible to claim that anything that makes one feel better is in some way a gift of God. We cannot quarrel with so broad an interpretation of the meaning of 'gift'.

But we believe it is the *use* of glossolalia that determines whether or not it is a constructive phenomenon or rather damages and destroys. Glosso-lalia rarely benefits a wide segment of the community.

We hope therefore that its practitioners as well as the scientists who study the phenomenon will be modest in their claims for it. For it is not uniquely spiritual; it is not uniquely the result of God's intervention in man's speech. Whether or not it is a gift of God's providential care for his people depends on varying subjective interpretations of the nature of what is spiritual and what constitutes a good gift for man.[9]

Furthermore the Scriptures say emphatically that tongues are a sign not to believers but unbelievers. Paul quotes Isaiah (28:11,12) in his exposition of this subject (1 Cor. 14:21,22).

What about self-edification in tongue speaking? It is true that by this means one's spirit can be moved and uplifted but the mind is not instructed. Moreover there is no way in which one can prove that the exercise is not self-induced or psychological.

When we turn from the vocal gifts to the power gifts, the matter of healing miracles is most prominent. This subject is analysed by B. B. Warfield in his treatise *Counterfeit Miracles*. It is easy to dismiss the author for being negative but if one of our own relatives had suddenly to make the choice between dependance on surgery or a miracle then Warfield's book would be extremely relevant. We would want to be every bit as careful and perceptive as he was.

The difference between the miracles of our Lord and his apostles and the majority of claims made today is that theirs took a matter of seconds whereas so many today seem to be long drawn out affairs.

I believe that God does intervene in an extraordinary way in some cases but like Ken Haarhof I have never come across a modern miracle that I could put into the same category as the New Testament miracles.

Either God has restored the gifts or he has not.   If he has, then these questions would not and could not be raised because the power would be beyond dispute.   We never read of anyone questioning the miracles of Jesus.   Some of his enemies attributed his power to Satan but no one doubted the authenticity of his miracles as such. The difficulty of authenticity is one which perplexes many.   So many claims simply lack the marks of authenticity.   When Jesus fed the multitudes there was no doubt about the miracle.   It was because he actually possessed power to create bread and fish that they tried to seize him to make him a king.

To sum up the main problem I would say that if God did enable real miracles to be performed today, such as would pass the test of the scrutiny of the newspapermen and television men, we would need to be very careful indeed in our evaluation of the purpose of such wonders.   We read of the fearful possibility of deception in Revelation 13:13,14 – of fire coming down from heaven in the sight of men, and of miracles.   If persuaded however that the wonders bore every mark of being of God we could interpret them as a demonstration of the reality of the supernatural in a materialistic age, or if to do with healing, a proof of God's compassion.   We would not conclude that Scripture needed any further authentication.   Nor would we conclude that now we must revert back to the extraordinary as the norm for the churches.

3. *The dangers of the Charismatic experience*

The first and most obvious danger connected with having or receiving something special is the sin of pride.   Even the mighty Paul received a thorn in the flesh to ensure that he should not fall into this trap.   'And lest I should be exalted above measure through the abundance of the revelations there was given to me a thorn in the flesh' (2 Cor. 12:7).   Pride is the first danger.   The second is to put experience before truth.   All experience must be subservient to the discipline of Scripture.   The third danger is to become preoccupied with experiences.   The fourth danger is to use the Charismatic experience to promote false unity.

1. *The danger of pride*

At one time John Wesley found it necessary to write to a certain Miss Bolton as follows: 'George Bell, William Green and others, then full of love, were favoured with extraordinary revelations and manifestations from God.   But by this very thing, Satan beguiled them from the simplicity of life in Christ.   By insensible degrees they were led to value these extraordinary gifts more than the ordinary grace of God: this, my dear friend, makes me fear for you. . . .'

J. Grant Shank, Jr., writing in *Christianity Today*[10] described the arrival and departure from his church of a group of a dozen tongue-speakers.   Grant Shank, pastor of a Nazarene church (a group that maintains second blessing and Arminian teaching) gave these friends a warm welcome.   There were smiles all round, hand-shakes and the familiar expression, much repeated, 'praise the Lord!'   After several months, relates Shank, it was obvious that these newcomers regarded themselves as spiritually superior with a 'know-it-all' attitude giving the impression that the non-glossolalia members had not 'arrived' spiritually speaking.   This seemed to blind them to the fact that there were serious deficiencies in their own lives in the area of disciplined living.

It might be helpful to pause at this stage to point out that, while many pastors throughout the world could relate the divisive effects of what we are describing, it does not follow that all tongue-speakers are necessarily like those who arrived at pastor Shank's church.   As we have seen, the 'supersaints' are not only to be found among the Charismatics.   A superiority complex was rife among the Pharisees of Jesus' day and brands of spiritual pride have persisted throughout the years.

But back to pastor Shank, who was deeply grieved.   He noted that 1 Corinthians 12 teaches unity and that whatever brings disunity is not to be tolerated.   He could see a split coming in his church and after doing his best to offer a basis of cordiality and understanding with the tongue-speakers he was compelled to admit defeat.   He had hoped that the additions would be a blessing to the assembly and result in soul-winning but he came reluctantly to the firm conclusion that the tongue-speakers 'did not have the Holy Spirit'.   They were possessed with a counterfeit, a fake.   They were living on an ego trip, a manufactured religious 'High'. The daily lives of these people did not match their witness, and so they hurt him, the congregation, and their own testimony as well as the cause of Jesus Christ.

The tongue-speakers left for another church but pastor Shank has noted that these people become 'church hoppers' and when they move on they do not hesitate to take people with them and when they have left 'they criticise with barbed speech persons in the previous church'.

Happily pastor Shank does not reveal a bitterness or over-reaction. Church leaders in particular should never allow themselves to be moved from or pushed off their settled doctrinal convictions by the extremes of others. They must be immovable. Setbacks must only make them more determined and firm in the truth. Moses was not moved by the provocative and rebellious cries of a crazy and carnal multitude. At one point he did allow himself to lose his temper. He spoke rashly and God punished him very severely for his sin. He had no excuse because he knew better, God having equipped him and placed him in that very place of responsibility that he might keep cool and see through the mammoth task of sanctification of a whole people in the wilderness.

2. *Experience must not be placed before truth*

Why has the Charismatic Movement outside the Roman Catholic Church found affinity and unity with the Charismatics inside the Roman Catholic Church? Why is it that Charismatics within the Roman Catholic Church do not embrace the great doctrines of justification by faith alone and salvation by grace alone. Why? Why is it that they say, as Herbert Carson documents in his up-to-date study of the Church of Rome with the thought provoking title of *Dawn or Twilight* (I.V.P.) that the Charismatic experience causes them to appreciate the mass more? The answer to these questions is that when religion is based on experience or sanctification as the foundation there can be no substantial progress. I believe that it is of the utmost importance that we understand, the Reformation and the main issue that was at stake then, and which continues to be the vital issue today.

The sixteenth century Reformation was an event which led to the regaining of the Bible for the world and the deliverance of the nations from darkness and superstition. What happened is that the re-formers regained the doctrine of Christ and his apostles and reasserted it, putting it back in its rightful place. Justification by faith was enthroned in its biblical position and properly related to the doctrine of sanctification like this:

1. The Gospel of justification by faith
———————————————————————
2. The experience of sanctification

or put in another way:

1. What God has done outside of us and for us in Christ
———————————————————————
2. What God achieves inside us as a result of the above

If we invert the order like this:

1. Our experience
———————————————
2. Justification by faith

then justification is going to be like a golden coin which gets lost at the bottom of a pool of religious experience which becomes more and more confused. This is exactly what happened in the twelve hundred years of darkness between the first three centuries following the apostolic era and the sixteenth century reformation. Whatever happens we must not return to another dark age. This will undoubtedly occur if we do not keep justification by faith in its rightful place.

Luther stated it well when he said, 'If the article of justification is lost, all Christian doctrine is lost at the same time . . . it alone makes a person a theologian . . . for with it comes the Holy Spirit, who enlightens the heart by it and keeps it in the true certain understanding so that it is able precisely and plainly to distinguish and judge all other articles of faith, and forcefully to sustain them.'[11]

If ever a truth needed to be engraven upon our very beings as Christians it is the sum and substance of the first chapters of Romans. The elements of this truth of justification are beautifully and succinctly brought together and expressed in the Westminster larger Catechism:

What is justification?

Justification is an act of God's free grace to sinners, in which he pardons all their sins, accepts and accounts their persons as righteous in his sight:

not for anything wrought in them, or done by them, but only for the perfect obedience and full satisfaction of Christ, by God imputed to them, and received by faith alone.

The primacy and meaning of Justification and its relationship to experience is brought out clearly when we see Justification contrasted with Sanctification as follows:

JUSTIFICATION	SANCTIFICATION
Is God's external work outside us and for us	Is God's internal work inside us
Is God's reckoning sinners to be righteous	Is God making sinners holy in heart and conduct
Is complete and perfect	Is never complete or perfect in this life
Is never subject to increase	Is a work of increase and progress
Is the foundation of our acceptance with God	Is a work God does in us because he has accepted us
Is a gift which entitles us to heaven	Is a work within which prepares us for heaven
Is a legal act which takes into account Christ's good works but has no regard for ours whatsoever	Is a spiritual work enabling believers to be active in good works

If the truth expressed in column two is placed before that of column one chaos results. Our Christianity must be firmly based upon what God has done for us and not be centred on what is going on inside us. Both justification and sanctification are essential to salvation. Both are the gift of God. Both proceed on the basis of union with Christ, both begin at the same time. But justification must always be the starting point and the foundation.

3. Preoccupation with experience

During 1977 a believer described two revivals which he had witnessed in Borneo. The first was classical in the sense that it was typical of revivals down through the centuries. Preaching, conviction of sin, repentance and transformation of life were the predominating features.   The second revival which followed a couple of years later was Charismatic in character.   The speaker himself reflected the impact that the second revival had made upon him personally.   He gave description after description of visions, exorcisms, healings, spirit baptisms and sensational events such as preservation in the jungle and the moving of lights in meetings.   One felt while listening to this account that the Word of God had been supplanted by all the externals.   It is possible to become so enamoured with the extraordinary and with excitements and sensational happenings that such matters become the daily diet of believers.   Eventually it is all they can talk about which is the hallmark of most Charismatic books.[12]   Scripture is supplanted by the narration of events which goes on ad infinitum.

When Peter got up to preach at Pentecost he did not launch into detailed descriptions of the amazing and unique experience they had just been through.   He preached salvation.

Someone might say that things in England are so dull, orthodox, staid, ordinary and dead that an afternoon's worth of the extraordinary and the exciting could do a lot of good and redress the balance.   It is true that information is necessary and worthwhile but whether the recounting of such events is encouraging to weary ministers is another matter.   We have no shortage of people who can recount their Charismatic experiences over and over again but their lives are in a sorry state.   To persuade such to live by the Word rather than by dependence on their experiences is an extremely difficult task.   To think of a whole multitude of people newly converted through a gracious revival is superlatively wonderful.   But to hear of the same people falling into the trap of preoccupation with extraordinary experiences is discouraging.

As Jonathan Edwards was God's wonderful gift to the eighteenth century Awakening, to encourage growth in grace and discipline, and discourage preoccupation with the externals, in like manner a gift of that kind to Borneo at this time would be invaluable.

4. *Using the Charismatic experience to promote false unity*

The modern Pentecostal movement is claimed to be the greatest ecstatic movement in the history of the Christian Church.   Commencing at the turn of the century it began to enter the mainstream denominations in the 1950's.   During the 1960's the movement surged forward.   This is illustrated by the case of the Evangelical Anglicans in England.   In their great get-together at Keele in 1967 the Charismatics were still on the fringe and regarded with much suspicion. Ten years later at the National Evangelical Anglican Conference held at Nottingham they formed a substantial proportion of the whole body with one of their leaders, David Watson of York extolling the achievement of unity with Roman Catholics and saying that 'in many ways the Reformation was one of the greatest tragedies that ever happened to the Church'.[13] Another Charismatic leader, Michael Harper, takes the same line (almost as though he had been briefed by the Vatican as to his wording) when he talks about 'tearing apart the Body of Christ'.[14] By what stretch of the imagination could the pre-Reformation Church be equated with 'the Body of Christ'?

The Charismatic movement has entered such Protestant churches as the Episcopal, Lutheran and Presbyterian bodies. We see that in about 1967 the movement was commenced in the Roman Catholic Church and since 1971 has made progress in the Greek Orthodox Church.

The similar experiences shared by those of differing denominations has led to public declarations such as the official statement of the second National Evangelical Anglican Congress which says, 'Seeing ourselves and Roman Catholics as fellow Christians, we repent of attitudes that have seemed to deny it' (Mlb). The clause just quoted follows recognition of the movement for renewal in the Roman Catholic Church (Mla), and later is qualified by an affirmation that the major issues of the Reformation are still regarded as crucial (Mlf).

To break out of the straitjacket that has existed for centuries is a very exciting prospect. To see Cardinal Suenens, Briege McKenna (a Franciscan nun), Andrew Morton of the British Council of churches, Tom Smail and Michael Harper rejoicing together might too easily lead us to conclude that this is a superlative breakthrough! The grim truth is however that Roman Catholic dogma and Roman Catholic authority have not changed one iota. Rome retains her facility to absorb political and religious elements of all kinds.

Love is essential (1 Corinthians 13) but truth is equally essential.

Paul insisted on a clearly stated, defined Gospel and with regard to the primacy and necessity of Justification by faith he allowed for no compromise of any kind. The first chapter of Galatians makes this very plain. Even if a darling angel, the best, sweetest and most lovable that ever the world saw, came and united with us in the most ecstatic love experience of Jesus ever known—if that same angel went on and preached a doctrine that contradicted Justification by faith alone for salvation then the very strongest curse of God would be upon him.   To that curse we would all be required to give our most hearty assent and approval and withdraw completely from that angel.   A favourite song among the Charismatics is the hymn 'Jesus is Lord'.   Jesus is Lord indeed.   He has been exalted, crowned, celebrated and is adulated because he has procured our justification by the agonies on the cross.   Any obscuring of that, his greatest achievement, is to defame his glory.   If *experience* is permitted to gobble up *doctrine*, if *love* is allowed to devour *principle*, if *sentiment* is suffered to obscure *justification by faith only*—then how will the world's multitudes be saved?   How can Jesus be Lord for them? Satan will continue to have his dominion over them.   Those who are ready to unite on the basis of love and common Charismatic experience at the expense of Justification should remember that in doing so they will be celebrating the lordship of Satan, not the Lordship of Christ.

FOOTNOTES

[1] February 28, 1975.   A profile of the Charismatic Movement.
[2] p. 17 *Reflected Glory* as published by Hodder, a 156 page small size paperback, 85p. Thomas A. Smail is the director of the Fountain Trust.   He is a self-confessed Barthian. His doctrine of the person of Christ is heretical, cf. p. 66ff.
[3] Quoted from an article on Christmas Evans by Robert Oliver in *Reformation Today*, issue 29.
[4] ibid. p. 44.
[5] *Counterfeit Miracles*, p. 25ff.
[6] *Reformation Today*, issue 16.
[7] See John Owen on schism, vol. 14 p. 364.   Also see helpful article on this subject by Bill Payne, *Reformation Today*, issue 33.
[8] Quoted from a tape-recorded message by George Gardiner of U.S.A.
[9] *The Psychology of Speaking in Tongues*, John P. Kildahl, 1972, Hodder, p. 86.
[10] ibid.
[11] *What Luther Says*, vol. 2 pp. 702-714, 715-718.
[12] An example of this is Demos Shakarian's, *The Happiest People on Earth*, as told to John and Elizabeth Sherrill.
[13] This statement made a powerful impact and was reported in the *Church of England's* newspaper daily report for NEAC.   Correspondence between David Watson and the author was published in *Reformation Today*, issue 38.
[14] *Let My People Grow*, p. 111.

Chapter 5

The Free Grace Experience

THE free grace experience is the most glorious, deepest or most profound, the richest, most fruitful and enduring experience of all.

It is the most glorious experience because like nothing else in the universe it redounds to the glory of Father, Son and Holy Spirit. It is the deepest or most profound because we can only wonder at, but never understand why we who are so unworthy should have free favour heaped upon us.

It is the richest experience because it promotes in us worship, adoration, praise and gratitude. It is the most fruitful as it leads to and encourages sustained devoted service. It explains why Paul laboured more than any other.

Free grace is the most enduring experience. It is never-ending. Our admiration of free grace will abound for ever and ever.

All God's attributes are glorious and all excite our admiration. His justice and holiness shine and adorn all his other attributes. His power and wisdom are marvellous. His love is astonishing. But were it not for grace or free favour we would receive nothing. An understanding and experience of undeserved free favour impresses the heart with indelible impressions. It casts light upon and gives perspective to the whole of salvation which it explains from beginning to end. The truth of free grace ensures that from start to finish all honour and glory is ascribed to the Triune God.

> *Grace all the work shall crown,*
> *Through everlasting days;*
> *It lays in heaven the topmost stone,*
> *And well deserves the praise.*

This verse by Doddridge and Toplady reminds us of Zechariah's prophecy. Zerubbabel would complete all his work in Jerusalem and when the topmost stone of the Temple was laid the people would shout, 'Grace, Grace to it' (Zech. 4:7).

Every aspect of the restoration of the Commonwealth of Israel at that time came through grace.

So it is with our personal salvation. From the first stirrings of conscience to our coming to Christ and our being kept right through to that great day of triumph, the resurrection, all is of grace. Then in the ages to come we will go on receiving generous expressions of God's loving-kindness. No sentence could sum it up better than that of Paul. All is to the praise of the glory of his grace (Eph. 1:6).

I have used superlative expressions to describe free grace. What does it mean?

The meaning of free grace

The Hebrew word grace (chen) in the Old Testament denotes the favour of God exercised toward the unworthy. This favour is voluntary and under no constraint or obligation. For instance out of mankind determined as a whole to follow the path of destruction, Noah was chosen to receive favour (grace) from God which saved both him and his family. The exercise of such favour or goodwill excites wonder and admiration. It is a thing of beauty.

To be gracious (charizomai) in the New Testament signifies the giving of favour, to show kindness or to pardon. The noun (charis) means favour or goodwill. The word was often used to describe the quality or virtue of the one bestowing such favour and implied beauty in that person. In Greek mythology Charis was the name given to the exceedingly beautiful wife of Hephaestos. One infinitely beautiful in a unique sense is the person of God's Son who is full of grace and truth. The word grace signifies sheer beauty.

The New Testament which employs the noun 150 times leaves us without any doubt about the meaning of grace. Grace is an attribute of God, the exercise of which lays hold of sinners and secures their salvation in Christ. Grace is the exercise of God's free favour. 'By grace ye are saved through faith; and that not of yourselves: it is the gift of God; Not of works lest any man should boast. For we are his workmanship, created in Christ Jesus unto good works, which God hath before ordained that we should walk in them' (Eph. 2:8-10).

This statement taken within its context shows God's grace to be the sole reason for our having been raised up out of spiritual death. We were spiritually dead. A resurrection was essential. The life given in the first instance and the good works we are now able to perform are all the result of God's favour. In the ages to come, that is, in all future time, the 'exceeding riches of his grace' will be displayed, appreciated and admired (Eph. 2:7).

Imagine two very rich men. When requested to donate toward a very worthy cause both give of their riches. The first one donates one hundred pounds, but the other gives a million pounds. The first gives *of* his riches, the second *according to* his riches. But how are we to measure God's grace? Who can measure it? Ours was not a worthy cause. We did not have merit but demerit. The grace God bestows upon the unworthy is described as superabundant, excelling or surpassing. It is shown in his kindness toward us through Christ. It is by and through him who is our righteousness that grace reigns even to eternal life. Sin is pictured as an absolute monarch exercising complete sovereignty (Rom. 5:21). Grace also reigns. As Abraham Booth expressed it in his classic *The Reign of Grace*, grace reigns in our election, calling, forgiveness, justification, adoption, sanctification and perseverance.

When grace is spoken of as free – 'being justified freely by his grace' (Rom. 3:24) – it means that it is an act of God's will which is free of any constraints, pressures or obligations. He is not obliged to do anything at all. No deservings or merits whatsoever come under consideration. This is illustrated by the parable of two debtors of whom our Lord said, 'and when they had nothing to pay, he frankly forgave them both' (Luke 7:42). They could make no claim but only appeal for mercy. Nor should the appeal for mercy in itself be viewed as a human merit because all our Godward desires owe their origin to his drawings. Thus when God describes his dealings with Jews he says that the goodness he showed to them was not for anything in them, 'Not for your sakes do I this, saith The Lord God, be it known unto you, O house of Israel, but for mine holy name's sake' (Ez. 36:22,32).

Grace is ascribed to the Father, the Son and the Holy Spirit.

Paul begins all his epistles by commending the readers to the grace of the Father which is seen in the fact that he has blessed us with all spiritual blessings. It is because of the Father's love that he has chosen a people and given them to his Son. This love is a love surpassing description. To be the subject of such love is to be the recipient of grace or favour which is immeasurable. Such was this love and the free grace motivating the Father to exercise it that he gave his Son to procure redemption. It is the Father's good pleasure not only to give his Son to redeem his people (he shall save his people from their sins) but to give them the Kingdom (Matt. 1:23, Luke 12:32). The extent of the Father's grace is seen in that he was careful to predestinate that everything should work for their good. His free favour toward his children is rich and comprehensive. His care for them is meticulous and is given with perfect wisdom.

The grace of the Father is described as a free grace but sometimes also as *sovereign*. He is the sovereign in the choice of those upon whom he wills to give Salvation. 'I will have mercy upon whom I will have mercy' (Rom. 9:15). The exercise of sovereign grace was referred to by our Lord when he said, 'I thank thee, O Father, Lord of heaven and earth, because thou hast hid these things from the wise and prudent, and hast revealed them to babes. Even so, Father: for so it seemed good in thy sight' (Luke 10:21). The occasion of this saying was when the seventy returned from their mission. They rejoiced in their gifts and power to cast out devils. He told them to rejoice rather in the sovereign grace of God. 'Rejoice,' he says, 'because your names are written in heaven.' Sovereign grace means that the Father alone is responsible for our names being written there. The choice we made for ourselves was hell. The choice he made for us was heaven. He sovereignly overruled our wretched choice by his choice and determination to bring us home to himself through grace.

The grace of the Son can be seen in the whole of his life and work on our behalf. 'For you know the grace of our Lord Jesus Christ, that, though he was rich, yet for your sakes he became poor that we through his poverty might be rich' (2 Cor. 8:9). That is a beautiful summary of the way in which God's grace has come to us. All grace that we receive is mediated through the person and work of Christ.

When the Scriptures conclude with the words 'The grace of our Lord Jesus Christ be with you all' (Rev. 22:21) it summarizes that which has been done for God's people and that which continues to be theirs. God's favour in, through and by Christ continues to rest with them. This is the wish and prayer frequently expressed by Paul at the conclusion of his letters.

The Holy Spirit who applies God's grace or favour is called the Spirit of grace (Zech. 12:10). His great work is to regenerate and sanctify God's elect. This raises the very important distinction that exists between sovereign, effectual grace and common or general grace.

When God's attributes of goodness are celebrated in Psalm 145 the Psalmist quotes the revelation that God made of himself to Moses (Ex. 34:6,7). God's grace as expressed to all the world is praised. His goodness is shown to all, and his tender mercies over all his works. This general favour or common grace is something too easily taken for granted. There was no favour shown to the fallen angels. God was not obliged to show rebels grace. Nor was he obliged to bestow favour upon a race that had sided with a race of rebel angels. But he did show grace to mankind in general by granting a period of probation in which they might repent.

Common grace is God's attitude of good will towards his enemies in which he shows much goodness, longsuffering and forbearance with a view to their repentance (Rom. 2:4, 2 Pet. 3:9). Evil in the world is restrained on a vast scale by the exercise of the Holy Spirit (Gen. 6:3), by the provision of civil governments (Rom. 13: 1-4) and by the provision of family life. Not only does God restrain evil, he positively bestows enormous good by way of human gifts and talents, by the sciences, by innumerable benevolent institutions and abounding provisions made to meet human need. All this undeserved favour is usually referred to as common grace. But this grace does not save. It does not apply the blood of Christ to sinners. It does not regenerate. It must be carefully distinguished from the free grace of God which is the exercise of God's power in calling out an elect people for himself.

The experience of free grace

In times of revival sinners experience a deep conviction of their sinful condition. Sometimes this experience can be agonizing. As souls first discover their appalling condition of lostness and guilt and then are led to search for and find salvation by faith in Christ, the glory of God's grace shines resplendently. The hymns which stem from revival times well express admiration for God's saving grace. Well known is John Newton's expression of gratitude,

Amazing grace (how sweet the sound)
That saved a wretch like me!
I once was lost, but now am found:
Was blind, but now I see.

Observe the sense of former wretchedness, lostness and blindness and the overwhelming sense of joy and praise that follows.

We are certainly not living in times of spiritual awakening today and we find that most believers came to salvation without deep, protracted or profound conviction of sin.

When people come easily to Christ their appreciation is not always very strong and there can be a tendency to take things for granted. A shallow experience is reflected in an unwillingness to sacrifice or to serve. Little enthusiasm is shown about prayer meetings or worship services. Behind this easy-going and often lukewarm attitude is the simple philosophy that God has given everyone in the world an equal chance or opportunity to be saved. By his Spirit, so the idea goes, he enables all to have a free choice. Those who exercise faith are saved and those who do not are lost. It is all very matter of fact.

The teaching of free grace explodes this easy-going philosophy as false. In its place the truth is established that men by nature do not choose God; he chooses them, predestinates them, calls them, justifies them and infallibly brings them home to glory.

The meaning of what has just been said is alarming to the easy-going Christian who believes that it is his faith which makes the difference between him and the lost. That is true in one sense. But where did faith come from? It is God's gift (Heb. 12:2, 2 Pet. 1:1, Eph. 2:8,9). Now in order to preserve a place for human merit (albeit a tiny bit) some will argue at great length that the Holy Spirit helps people to faith so that it is a combination of human effort and divine enablement.

The Holy Spirit's method of bringing believers to free grace is by causing them to experience conviction of sin and need. For instance it was when Jonah came to see that there was no way out of the fish that he exclaimed, 'Salvation is of the Lord' (Jonah 2:9).

By conviction of sin the sinner realizes that he would never have come himself. His will was not free. His will was in bondage. Several main Scripture passages such as Romans 3 confirm that none seeks after God by nature. Salvation is not only provided. It is applied by God as he calls people to himself.

After a prolonged time of deep conviction Spurgeon came to embrace free grace. He describes his experience as follows:

Well can I remember the manner in which I learned the doctrines of grace in a single instant. Born, as all of us are by nature, an Arminian, I still believed the old things I had heard continually from the pulpit, and did not see the grace of God. When I was coming to Christ, I thought I was doing it all myself, and though I sought the Lord earnestly, I had no idea the Lord was seeking me. I do not think the young convert is at first aware of this. I can recall the very day and hour when first I received those truths in my own soul – when they were, as John Bunyan says, burnt into my heart as with a hot iron, and I can recollect how I felt that I had grown on a sudden from a babe into a man – that I had made progress in Scriptural knowledge, through having found once for all, the clue to the truth of God. One week-night, when I was sitting in the house of God, I was not thinking much about the preacher's sermon for I did not believe it. The thought struck me, 'How did you come to be a Christian?' I sought the Lord. 'But how did you come to seek the Lord?' The truth flashed across my mind in a moment – I should not have sought Him unless there had been some previous influence in my mind to make me seek Him. I prayed, thought I, but then I asked myself, How came I to pray? I was induced to pray by reading the Scriptures. How came I to read the Scriptures? I did read them, but what led me to do so? Then in a moment I saw that God was at the bottom of it all, and that He was the Author of my faith, and so the whole doctrine of grace opened up to me, and from that doctrine I have not departed to this day, and I desire to make this my constant confession, 'I ascribe my change wholly to God.'

Lying at the heart and core of the lives, motivation and ministries of the outstanding Christians of the age is a passionate appreciation of free grace. That Peter should be restored after such a dismal failure was due to grace. Peter's conviction of his unworthiness was intense, and his subsequent devotion commensurately so.

That Paul should receive grace and apostleship when his activities as a persecutor warranted nothing but wrath gave him a sense of indebtedness to which he constantly testified in his preaching and writings.

The sixteenth century Reformation began in the heart of Luther. His was a free grace experience born out of a tremendous struggle in which he came to see that salvation was not by free will but by grace alone.

George Whitefield tells of how he came to experience free grace as a young man aged twenty-four. This was during a sea voyage to America. As an immensely successful preacher the temptation to pride was as wide as the sea and sky around him for there was no preacher as able as he. Yet it was then that he was overcome by conviction of sin and a wretchedness so intense that he even contemplated giving up the ministry. This time of conviction, according to his own testimony, helped him to understand the doctrines of grace: election and adoption.   This experience of humbling served to deepen and strengthen him and cause him to lean more upon God. This was not the last time Whitefield was to experience such conviction.

We must not think that this kind of experience belongs to the archives of church history, something confined to a past age.   The story of Drew Garner and his wife Frances furnish us with one example of many multiplying throughout the world today.   Drew Garner was a young pastor of a large Southern Baptist Church with about one thousand members.   Behind an impressive facade of highly organised and efficient evangelical activity lay a disillusioned and theologically disorientated pastor.   Drew confesses that he was far along the road of liberalism in his heart and heading straight in the direction of total scepticism and abandonment of the faith.   Nevertheless the machinery had to be kept going, and the machinery also kept him going.

One Sunday he was tipped off to visit a newcomer into the area who might, if visited, be drawn to swell the ranks of the church. Southern Baptists do not generally lack in speed of movement when it comes to making additions to their churches.   Early Monday morning Drew knocked on the door.   In his own words, 'the ugliest man I have ever seen appeared unshaven and in his dressing gown'.   The man informed Drew that there was time only for a few words.

'Do you make altar calls?' the ugly man growled.

'Of course I do,' said Drew.

'Why do you make them?'

'To give people a chance to decide!'

'Do you think people have to have a chance?   Does God save by chance?

Just as Drew began to think, 'what kind of a nut have I got on my hands' the ugly man said, 'I would like for you to see my library'. He showed Drew inside.   A magnificent array of Puritan books was unveiled before Drew.   Although at sea theologically, Drew had been well educated.   He knew instinctively that he was with someone who knew what he believed, who studied those books, and who was well grounded in Christian doctrine and life.   Bringing the short meeting to a close the ugly man said, 'I want you to read two books'.   He gave him Pink's *The Sovereignty of God* and Loraine Boettner's *Predestination*.

Drew made a few more calls and returned home.   'A strange man called this morning on his way to work,' said Frances. 'He said he was new to the area and that he would like me to read John chapter six.' 'Was he a big ugly man?' asked Drew. 'Yes,' replied Frances. 'He's a nut!' said Drew, and went into his study.

Sitting down the old familiar feeling of theological desolation came upon him. He had run dry and was desperate. Apart from evangelical gimmickry he was doctrinally and spiritually bankrupt. His eyes fell upon the two books he had brought in. He began to read.

The ugly man dropped in next day to see Frances about her progress in John six. Her studies were going well and by Wednesday she was breaking up. On Thursday Drew's reading of the two books brought him suddenly and dramatically to the point of revelation. Suddenly his eyes were opened! He saw it all in an instant! Leaping in the air he shouted as loud as it is possible for a man to shout. The whole plan of God, his sovereignty and his purpose had fallen into place. He rushed out to share it with Frances. She too had seen it. They rejoiced together. Life had begun anew. The theological desert, the barren spiritual wandering, the doubt and scepticism had all gone, and gone forever. A new life had begun.

The future years were to prove hard but rewarding. Drew Garner has never ceased to thank God for sending that excellent man and using him so decisively. In the place of evangelical tradition has come a full and rich ministry not only in the realm of soulwinning and evangelism but in pastoral work and church planting.

The blessings that result from the free grace experience are many. It is a great help to have a strong, clear grasp of God's overall plan of salvation. To be able to understand theology and rejoice in God's sovereign purpose as it is unfolded in Scripture is most helpful. As we have just seen in the case of Drew Garner, doubt was expelled. Clarity and strength of faith replaced uncertainty and doctrinal ineptitude. A potent grasp of the truth accompanied with joy in the knowledge that it is *the* truth revealed by the Holy Spirit can transform a man's entire ministry. This was Drew Garner's experience. The change in his life is typical. Yet in my opinion humility is really first among the benefits that result from the free grace experience.

Humiliation as an experience is fundamental and indispensable to true Christianity, for of such evangelical humiliation come two essential attributes, namely, the fear of God and humility.

The fear of the Lord receives little if any attention in evangelical circles today.

We still have the phrase, 'a God-fearing man', although it is not used as much as it used to be.   The fear of God lies at the very heart of true Christianity.   Both Old and New Testaments speak much of this fear.   Indeed, there are hundreds of direct or indirect references to this matter in Scripture.   One of our most able modern preachers has well said: 'Take away the soul from the body and all you have left in a few days is a stinking carcase.   Take away the fear of God from any expression of godliness and all you have left is the stinking carcase of Pharisaism and barren religiosity'. We would go further and say that the most excited and enthusiastic expressions of religion: shouting, raising of hands, singing of choruses, intense speech, praying all at the same time, exuberant laughings or sad wailings, if devoid of a true fear of God, are all revolting in the extreme especially to those who have come to experience the fear of God.   How does one discern a true fear of the Lord?   The answer is that it is accompanied by a reverence for Scripture, a repudiation of all lightness, frivolity and flippancy, a conformity of heart to the precepts of the Word.   A true fear of the Lord is often experienced in awful stillness: 'Be still and know that I am God' (Ps. 46:10). Such a fear leads to a thoughtful and living relationship with God in which those beautiful attributes described by our Lord in the sermon on the mount are developed, namely, sorrow for sin, meekness, purity, mercy, peacemaking and joy (Matt. 5:1-12).

One of the practical effects of the fear of God is humility.   The Prodigal Son was brought to humiliation.   He soon squandered his substance and his gifts of character, thus bringing himself both to profligacy and penury.   The backward slide was permitted in order to bring him to an end of himself.   He showed true repentance when he determined to return to his father.   That he was humbled was seen in his words, 'Father I have sinned against heaven and in thy sight, and am no more worthy to be called thy son'.   The case of the Prodigal illustrates well God's purpose in the humbling of all his people.   Can you think of one saved character in Scripture who was not humbled?

The free grace experience not only results in the fear of God and true humility but it also brings about a new attitude about assurance. This is discussed later.   Enough to say here that the first consideration in assurance is objective – that is a knowledge that God has given us the Holy Spirit to witness in our hearts that we are children of God.

Free grace causes us to leave every reliance upon ourselves or dependence on what we have done and to look to the Lord alone to save us. We see that 'it is not of him that willeth, or of him that runneth but of God who sheweth mercy' (Rom. 9:16).

> *Nothing in my hand I bring,*
> *Simply to Thy cross I cling;*
> *Naked, come to Thee for dress,*
> *Helpless, look to Thee for grace;*
> *Foul! I to the fountain fly,*
> *Wash me, Saviour, or I die.*

Appreciation of free grace is the source of intense joy, a joy which inspires profound worship which is perhaps best expressed in the hymns we sing.

> *Sovereign grace o'er sin abounding,*
> *Ransomed souls, the tidings swell;*
> *'Tis a deep that knows no sounding;*
> *Who its breadth or length can tell?*
> *On its glories*
> *Let my soul for ever dwell.*

The fruit of the experience of free grace is rich; love, worship, gratitude, humility, joy, dedication, zeal, meekness, gentleness and compassion towards others. Those who have received so much so freely are the most thankful to God and the most ready to seek the good of others. Having so freely received they are the most zealous to give.

The dangers

What are the dangers of free grace? We considered the dangers of the Charismatic movement. Are there no perils for those who profess experience of sovereign grace?

There are several serious dangers. The first and most obvious is to rest in the experience and doctrine and to neglect the practical responsibilities of the faith. Another danger is to become sectarian about the matter. Even after fifteen years or more of renewed interest in free grace, those who put the doctrines into practice are still only a small minority among the wide family of believers. It is a temptation therefore to some to become negative and critical about those who do not accept free grace teaching and practice, and even to fall into the terrible sin of despising them. The Pharisees, we remember, fell into the sin of despising others.

There is also the danger too of becoming lop-sided or unbalanced by being hyper-intellectual as though reading free grace books was the alpha and omega of Christianity. Paul warned the Corinthians about knowledge which was not spiritual – a knowledge that puffed up (1 Cor. 8:1).

Then there is the most obvious danger of all which is to make the wrong conclusion that since grace is sovereignly given then we can leave it all to God and relax. The truth is that grace is given through human means. It is most significant that the truth of Romans which stresses the necessity of preaching the Gospel is found between the ninth and eleventh chapters which declare God's omnipotent sovereignty. Paul and the master he served both declared the sovereignty of God. Neither neglected the necessity of hard work and the maximum use of the means of grace by which sovereign grace comes to men.

Chapter 6

Conversion—the essential Experience

OF all experiences, conversion is most important. Without this experience we are lost and that for ever. If ever Christ was specific, it was on this issue. Said he, 'Except ye be converted – ye shall not enter into the kingdom of heaven' (Matt. 18:3).

By conversion is meant an about turn. Imagine a man on a beach facing the sea. If he keeps on walking until he can walk no more he will be buried in the ocean. If he does a one hundred and eighty degree turn and faces in exactly the opposite direction, he can begin to walk on dry land. Instead of an ocean the whole continent will be before him. When our Lord insists on a conversion he is of course insisting on a spiritual conversion which involves the leaving of an old world and an entrance into a new one. By turning in faith to Christ a man becomes a new creature. For him all things become new (2 Cor. 5:17).

The Christian experience of conversion is essential for salvation. Without it a person has no spiritual life. He remains in a lost state. Not only is conversion essential, but in itself it is profound and life-changing. This experience we call conversion changes a man for the rest of his life. Conversion can be sudden and dramatic as was the case with that persecutor Saul of Tarsus, or it can be sweet and gentle as was the case with Lydia. Lydia was a merchant-trader involved in the Jewish religion and she organised a regular little gathering for the purpose of prayer. It simply says of her that her heart was opened. In other words she just received the truth of the Gospel into her heart and forthwith acted in obedience to it. In the same city was another personality in the form of a rough man whose job it was to oversee the jail. An earthquake was used to awaken him and his experience of conversion was like an earthquake! In times of religious awakenings such conversions are frequent. We are not living in such times and most conversion experiences today are gradual and non-dramatic. The main point is not the drama or excitement but rather the reality of the faith involved. When a man has a true conversion experience he will never go back on what he believes. There is a saying that still waters run deep. Fireworks or drama in a conversion are not the only consideration. The proof of a man's conversion experience lies in the long testing time which follows.

When an unbeliever comes from a position of non-faith to faith, the strength of his faith will show in the extent of his commitment. A person who truly believes in the Gospel will obey its precepts. He will not be absent when the believers gather together. He will not lack enthusiasm in the worship of God or in his willingness to do good works, even though such may impose on time, energies and income. True faith will be seen by good works. It has been well said that Christianity in its wholeness can be likened to the human body in which proportion is essential. The head is first and is set on the shoulders. The mind or intellect being first, it rules and directs all the actions of the body. But a head severed from its body is monstrous and horrible. Then there is the whole cardio-vascular system which we sum up by the word heart but which an earlier English generation described as 'bowels'. In the Greek it simply means 'internals'. The word heart is frequently used to describe experience. What is the head without the cardio-vascular system and what are both without the limbs? Thought, experience and practice make up the Christian life in a beautiful proportion just as head, heart and limbs make up the human body.

Christians testify that they sometimes experience difficulty in maintaining a proper balance between the intellect, emotions and the practical work involved in church membership. Some find that they are too easily preoccupied with the intellect. They feel they can analyse everything but in a cold and clinical way. The neglect of the affections is perhaps the most common failing and not easy to remedy. What is your personal response to chapter 16 which is designed to provide a remedy? There are those who neglect their minds and become either too lazy or too busy to attend to disciplined study. And then there are the activists! In all their activities they fail both in worshipping God with all their minds as well as fail in their hearts.

Conversion involves the whole man. He is fully persuaded intellectually that the Bible is true, that Christ is divine, and that the resurrection, judgment and future world are realities. He feels about these things. They affect his experience and his will so that his limbs are brought into operation. His belief results in deeds, because he feels the importance of them and because he loves them. His will is moved by his heart and affections and his affections have been taught and enlightened by the mind.

The reason why some believers look with such disfavour on evangelistic appeals for people to come forward to profess faith, is that this method often succeeds in persuading people emotionally, as their minds are not persuaded, they soon fall away from their temporary profession. They have been subjected to emotional pressure and when the emotions pass there is nothing left. This may be one reason why it is often said of a new enthusiast for Christianity, 'It won't last long – it is a passing phase – give him a month, or, at the most, a year, and it will pass away!' In many cases it does pass away, just like the plants which our Lord described. They were on rocky ground and there was no depth of root in them. Happily there are those who are persuaded, not emotionally and temporarily, but wholly (mind, emotion and will) and who, therefore, endure to the end.

The lasting effects of the experience of conversion can be well seen in the case of Paul. Three detailed accounts of this important experience are provided in the book of Acts. The description itself is found in Acts 9:1-30. Paul gave a stirring narration of his conversion in public at Jerusalem (Acts 22:1-22) and again before a company convened by King Agrippa (Acts 26:1-30). The importance of this experience to Paul is impressed upon us by the fervour with which he describes what happened. As far as we can judge the power and glory of his conversion experience never left him. He seemed to be conscious of this himself (Col. 1:13ff; 1 Cor. 15:9ff).

The conversion of Paul was unique and exceptional. There is no other on record like it. It was exceptional inasmuch as a great light shone round about him, a voice spoke from heaven to him personally (while the others heard the sound, it was not intelligible to them, Acts 9:7 and 22:9) and an extraordinary physical effect came upon his eyes which lasted for three days.

While the conversion was unique and exceptional with regard to the circumstances, it was the same in its nature as every other conversion to Christ. The best summary, not only of Paul's conversion but of all conversions, is that in which he describes the event as the opening of the eyes, a turning from darkness to light, a deliverance from the power of Satan to God, a receiving of forgiveness of sin and an inheritance with others that cannot be taken away (Acts 26:18).

What a traumatic experience conversion is! Imagine being blind from birth, living like a slave in servitude, addicted to the practice of evil habits which increase one's sense of guilt without any prospect of release, and no hope of anything better. Imagine, then, someone coming to give you eyes to see the light and taking you by the hand to lead you to a new world of freedom and joy. At the same time you are given the assurance that your release and your newly-found possessions can never be taken away from you. Moreover, there are others who have received a similar deliverance and you are able to share the reality of it all with them.

What an experience!

Reader, have you been converted?

The about turn for Paul was immediate, total and final. Baptized three days after the Damascus-road experience he preached boldly in the city. He began at once to promote and exalt the very cause that he was formerly determined to root out and destroy. So zealously did he promote the kingdom of Christ that he brought upon himself the fury of his former associates. The persecutor became the persecuted. Being let down the Damascus wall in a basket, he returned to Jerusalem and there proclaimed the Faith he had formerly tried to destroy. Little wonder that fierce opposition was aroused. Of the success or otherwise of these first efforts we know little. Of Paul's later work, the winning of innumerable souls and the establishment of many churches we know much. The power of Christ which marked his conversion seems to be stamped upon all that he did subsequently. The powerful conversion experience made its impress upon the church of the apostolic era and has been a source of encouragement ever since.

The experience of conversion has lasting effects. We cannot forget the change. We cannot cease to be grateful for eyesight that can now see the celestial city and the king. Certainly, some conversion experiences are more powerful than others, but in most the conversion experience has a permeating and influential effect upon subsequent experience. This not only applies to the individual, but an impression is made upon the church of which he forms a part. New life and vigour is often brought to a languishing church by the conversion of a sinner.

I will conclude this chapter by recounting one of the most striking examples of a conversion experience and how it affected a whole church. Rolfe Barnard, who is regarded as a leading pioneer of free grace teaching during the barren years before the present awakening to the doctrines of grace, described a visit to a church in Canada where there had not been a single conversion for nine years! The church, he said was 'mighty orthodox and mighty separate!' When he arrived for a week of ministry he asked whether they had been out visiting people. The answer was no. He suggested that they ought to get acquainted with folks. Taking a deacon he began forthwith going from house to house. Eventually they came to a certain home, and as the preacher opened the gate to go in, the deacon said, 'I wouldn't go in there.'

'Why not?' asked the preacher.

'I wouldn't like to say,' replied the deacon, 'but I beg you not to go in there.'

'Well, I'm going,' insisted the preacher.

'Please don't go,' pleaded the deacon, 'it will ruin the meeting.'

'Why?' retorted the adamant preacher.

'Oh,' said the deacon, 'if you go in there it will be terrible. The most notorious woman in this part of Canada lives there!'

When the preacher arrived at the door an attractive woman, whose sinful life was not yet betrayed by her appearance, answered the door. Said the preacher, 'I am holding meetings and I have come to invite you to come and hear me preach tonight.'

The woman began to laugh and said, 'Are you really a preacher?'

'Yes,' he said, 'I am from the South and I am holding meetings in the church down the way.'

'Do you know who I am?' asked the woman.

'Yes!' replied the preacher, 'I have been told you are the most notorious woman in this section of Canada!'

'Yes,' she retorted, 'that is right, and you want *me* to come to that church building tonight?'

'Yes,' insisted the preacher, 'I double-dog dare you to come!'

'Why, if I came,' said she, 'I would shock them to death!'

'Maybe they need a shock down there, now then I want you to promise me you will come.'

She did come and as the time came to sing the last hymn she came running up to the front of the church and fell down before the preacher sobbing as though her heart would break. Movingly and quietly the congregation sang

Amazing grace (how sweet the sound)
That saved a wretch like me!
I once was lost, but now am found:
Was blind, but now I see.

This modern Magdalene rose to her feet, the glory of God shining on her countenance. As she just stood there one of the saintliest ladies of the church came down the aisle and embraced her, kissing her on both cheeks, exclaiming for all to hear, 'Welcome, sister!' At that moment the Holy Spirit came down and sinners all over the congregation began to call on God for mercy.

It was the beginning of a new era for that church – an era begun with the experience of conversion.

Unless you are converted, you will not enter the kingdom of heaven. Are you converted?

Chapter 7

Conversion—true or false?

THE order in which events occur in the salvation of a soul has always gripped theologians. What comes first the new birth or faith and repentance? A soul, dead toward God and wedded to a sinful life will not, and by reason of his bondage, cannot repent.

The Lord must take the initiative. Said our Lord, 'No man can come to me except the Father who sent me draws him.' Now this drawing can take place over a period of time, resulting in the new birth.

Students of the Bible have never agreed as to how to determine precisely when the new birth takes place. Even the Puritans, who showed unrivalled knowledge of the Bible and of divinity as a whole, disagreed among themselves as to where to place the new birth, whether to place it early or late in the process of drawing. 'Preparationism,' that is how much preparation of the Holy Spirit precedes the act of new birth, was a subject about which they debated in detail.

We should not be surprised at this because our Lord emphasised that the work of the Holy Spirit in the new birth is mysterious. He likened it to the wind. Who knows where the wind has come from precisely? We may know there is a wind because we see the trees blown by it. We can judge the general direction of the wind but that is about all.

Allowance must be made in experience for what is called a prevenient work of grace. A prevenient work, as the name suggests, is a work before or preparatory to the new birth. The Holy Spirit uses means in regeneration. The means are the preaching, teaching and imbibing of the truth. 'He chose to give us birth through the word of truth,' says James, and Peter put it this way, 'Being born again, not of corruptible seed, but of incorruptible, by the word of God, which liveth and abideth for ever' (1 Peter 1:23).

Just how much can be done in the soul by the Holy Spirit of God which falls short of regeneration can be seen by weighing the following statement by John Owen, who, of all the Puritans would contend for first prize when it comes to deep thinking about the truths of the Gospel.

There are certain *internal spiritual effects* wrought in and upon the souls of men, whereof the word preached is the immediate instrumental cause, which ordinarily do precede the work of regeneration, or real conversion unto God.   And they are reducible unto three heads:
    1. *Illumination*; 2. *Conviction*; 3. *Reformation*.   The first of these respects the mind only; the second, the mind, conscience and affections; and the third, the life and conversion.

The writer of Hebrews demonstrates how a person can go a long way in the Christian way of life, yet fall short of regeneration.

It is impossible for those who have once been enlightened, who have tasted the heavenly gift, who have shared in the Holy Spirit, who have tasted the goodness of the word of God and the powers of the coming age, if they fall away, to be brought back to repentance, because to their loss they are crucifying the Son of God all over again and subjecting him to public disgrace (Heb. 6:4-6, N.I.V.).

We see then that there can be a work of persuasion which can fall short of true conversion.   Also we observe that a prevenient work of grace should not be mistaken for true conversion.   These principles can be illustrated by the conversion experiences of different Christians.   The experience of B. H. Carroll, who was born in 1843 in Mississippi, America, is not only an example of outstanding interest, but it highlights the principles in a gripping way.   B. H. Carroll became one of the finest Christian preachers and leaders that America has ever known.   You will enjoy his story which he describes himself.   As you read it you will see in the first instance an example of a forced or false conversion.   After that we have the exciting description of the real thing.

The testimony of B. H. Carroll as told by himself

There was a protracted meeting in our vicinity.   A great, mysterious influence swept over the community.   There was much excitement. Many people, old and young, joined the church and were baptized. Doubtless, in the beginning of the meetings, the conversions were what I would now call genuine. Afterward, many merely went with the tide. They went because others were going. Two things surprised me. First, that I did not share the interest or excitement. To me, it was a curious spectacle. The second was that so many people wanted me to join the church. I had manifested no special interest, except once or twice mechanically and experimentally. I had no conviction of sin. I had not felt lost and did not feel saved. First one and then another catechised me and that categorically. Thus: Don't you believe the Bible? Yes. Don't you believe in Jesus Christ? Y-e-s. Well, doesn't the Bible say that whosoever believes in Jesus Christ is saved? Yes. These answers were reported. Ought not such a one to join the church? Now came the pressure of well-meant but unwise persuasion. The whole thing would have been exposed if, when I presented myself for membership, I had been asked to tell my own story without prompting or leading questions. I did not have any to tell and would have told none.

Until after my baptism, everything seemed unreal, but walking home from the baptism, the revelation came. The vague infidelity of all of the past took positive shape, and would not down at my bidding. Truth was naked before me. I did not believe that the Bible was God's revelation. I did not believe its miracles and doctrines. I did not believe, in any true sense, in the divinity and vicarious sufferings of Jesus.

Joining the church, with its assumption of obligations, was a touchstone. I saw my real self. I knew that either I had no religion or it was not worth having. This certainty as to my state had no intermittence. I knew that its avowal would pain and horrify my family and the church, yet honesty required me to say something, and so I merely asked that the church withdraw from me on the ground that I was not converted. This was not granted because the brethren thought that I mistook temporary, mental depression, as a lack of conversion.

In a meeting in Texas, when I was fifteen years old, I was persuaded to retain my membership for further examination.

But now came another event, I shall not name it. It came from no sin on my part but it blasted every hope and left me in Egyptian darkness. The battle of life was lost, in seeking the field of war, I sought death. By pre-emptory demand, I had my church connection dissolved and turned utterly away from every semblance of

Bible belief. In the hour of my darkness, I turned unreservedly to infidelity. As I was in the first Confederate regiment, so I was in the last corps that surrendered; and while armies grappled and throttled each other, a darker and deadlier warfare raged within me. Here now, was my case:

I turned my back on Christianity, and had found nothing in infidelity. Happiness was gone and death would not come. The Civil War had left me a wounded cripple, on crutches, utterly poverty-stricken and loaded with debt.

I had sworn never to put my foot into another church. My father died, believing me lost. My mother – when does a mother give up a child? – came to me and begged me for her sake that I would attend one more meeting. It was a Methodist camp meeting, held in the fall of 1865. I had not an atom of interest in it. I liked the singing, but the preaching did not touch me. But, the one day that I shall never forget – it was Sunday at 11.00, the great wooden shed was crowded. I stood on the outskirts, leaning on my crutches, wearily and somewhat scornfully enduring. The preacher made a failure, even for him. There was nothing in his sermon, but, when he came down, as I suppose to exhort as usual, he startled me, not only by not exhorting, but by asking some questions that seemed meant for me. He said, 'You that stand aloof from Christianity and scorn at simple folks, what have you got? Answer honestly before God. Have you found anything worth having where you are?' My heart answered in a moment. 'Nothing under the whole Heaven . . . absolutely nothing.' As if he had heard my unspoken answer, he continued, 'Is there anything else out there worth trying that has any promise in it?' Again, my heart answered, 'Nothing . . . absolutely nothing.' 'Well, then,' he continued, 'admitting there is nothing there, if there be a God, mustn't there be a something somewhere? If so, how do you know that it is not here? Are you willing to test it? Have you the fairness and courage to try it? I won't ask you to read any book nor study any evidences nor make any difficult and tedious pilgrimage; that takes too long and time is too short. Are you willing to try it now, to make a practical, experimental test? You are to be the judge of the result.'

These cool, calm, and pertinent questions hit me with tremendous force, but I did not understand them. He continued, 'I base my test on these two Scriptures. "If any man willeth to do his will, he shall know of the doctrine whether it be of God" (John 7:17). "Then shall we know, if we follow on to know the Lord" (Hosea 6:3).'

So, when he invited all who were willing to make an immediate, experimental test, to come forward and give him their hand, I immediately went forward. I was not prepared for the stir which this action created. My infidelity and my hostile attitude toward Christianity were so well known in the community that such action on my part developed quite a sensation. Some even began to shout, whereupon, to prevent any misconception, I arose and stated that I was not converted, that perhaps they misunderstood what was meant by my coming forward; that my heart was as cold as ice and that my action meant no more than that I was willing to make an experimental test of the truth and power of the Christian religion and that I was willing to persist in subjection to the test until a true solution could be found. This quieted matters.

The meeting closed without any change upon my part. The last sermon had been preached, the benediction had been pronounced, and the congregation was dispersing. A few ladies only remained seated near the pulpit, engaged in singing. Feeling that the experiment was ended and the solution was not found, I remained to hear them sing. As their last song, they sang:

> Oh land of rest, for thee I sigh, when will the moment come,
> When I shall lay my armour by and dwell in peace at home?

The singing made a wonderful impression upon me. Its tones were as soft as the rustling of angels' wings. Suddenly, there flashed upon my mind, like a light from Heaven, this Scripture, 'Come unto me, all ye that labour and are heavy laden and I will give you rest.' I did not see Jesus with my eye, but I seemed to see him standing before me, looking reproachfully and tenderly and pleadingly, seeming to rebuke me for having gone to all other sources for rest, but the right one, and now inviting me to come to him. In a moment, I went, once and forever, casting myself unreservedly and for all time at Christ's feet . . . and in a moment, the rest came, indescribable and unspeakable, and it has remained from that day until now.

I gave no public expression of the change which had passed over me, but spent the night in the enjoyment of it, and wondering if it would be with me when the morning came. When the morning came, it was still with me, brighter than the sunlight and sweeter than the song of birds, and now, for the first time, I understood the Scripture which I had often heard my mother repeat, 'Ye shall go out with joy, and be led forth with peace: the mountains and the hills shall break forth before you into singing, and all of the trees of the field shall clap their hands' (Isaiah 55:12).

When I reached home, I said nothing about the experience through which I had passed, hiding the righteousness of God in my heart; but it could not be hidden. As I was walking across the floor, on my crutches, an orphan-boy, whom my mother had raised, noted and called attention to the fact that I was both whistling and crying. I knew that my mother heard him and to avoid observation, I went at once to my room, lay down on the bed and covered my face with my hands. I heard her coming. She pulled my hands away from my face and gazed long and steadfastly upon me, without a word. A light came over her face that seemed to me as the shining on the face of Stephen; and then, with trembling lips, she said, 'My son, you have found the Lord.' Her happiness was indescribable. I don't think that she slept that night. She seemed to fear that with sleep she might dream and awake to find that the glorious fact was but a vision of the night. I spent the night at her bedside, reading Bunyan's *Pilgrim's Progress*. I read it all that night, and when I came with the pilgrims to the Beulah Land, from which doubting castles could be seen no more forever, and which was in sight of the Heavenly City, and within sound of the heavenly music, my soul was filled with such a rapture and an ecstasy of joy as I had never before experienced. I knew then, as well as I know now, that I would preach; that it would be my life work; that I would have no other work.

And that is how it turned out to be. B. H. Carroll was a free-grace founder of the now enormous Southern Baptist Convention. Would that all Southern Baptists would study the example and teaching of their worthy founding father. His testimony teaches us to distinguish between true and false conversion, an urgent lesson required today!

Chapter 8

No Genuine Experience without the Law

THE essence of Christianity is humility. Proud sinners are humbled before their holy Creator. Their stony hearts are exchanged for tender hearts upon which God writes his law. The moral law is God's schoolmaster to bring us to his Son. After that, the same law remains our rule of life, a guide as to what is right or wrong. But never is the law to be a means by which the believer tries to gain justification before God.

The person who has no experience of God's law has no experience at all! That is a strong statement but not an overstatement for the simple reason that we can never separate God from his law. If God disregarded law he would cease to be just, and if he ceased to be just he would cease to be God. Those who think only in terms of God's love deceive themselves because love is the fulfilment of the law. God is love but love has no terms of reference or definition without justice, and virtue cannot exist without law.

The law is essential not only because it tells us about the true nature of God but because it alone can humble proud sinners. Pride invaded the hearts of our first parents. They imbibed the deception that the fruit would make them wiser than God. Ever since their fall their progeny have believed the same lie. They all think that they know better, and believe that somehow they will escape the sentence of eternal punishment. It takes omnipotent power to overthrow this pride of men. It takes divine wisdom to persuade man that he is a sinner. There is no fear of God before the eyes of a proud man. He clothes himself in his own righteousness and justifies himself by his own works. He feels no need of Christ and despises religion as something for weak people.

How is this position changed? How is an ungodly man brought

to humiliation because of his sin? The moral law impressed upon the conscience is God's way of conviction. Without coming to terms with God as he really is, there can never be any experience of guilt or sin. The Gospel is good news for sinners exclusively.

It is important that we always think of God as the eternal One, the unchangeable One who by infinite power upholds all the universe. He stands outside anything he has created, and being eternally self-sufficient does not need anything extra to make him happy. He is immutable in his perfections. He can never favour evil. By nature he finds sin to be revolting. The whole of his being is repulsed by it.

This holiness of God is expressed by the ten commandments. The time and way in which he gave those commandments show how important they are. No sooner had the nation emerged from Egypt than it was confronted by Mount Sinai. The way in which the moral law was given was designed to impress upon the people the significance of the law. This same law was inscribed upon tables of stone by God himself and was uttered audibly by him. We rightly think of all truth coming through or being mediated through the Lord Jesus Christ, but such is the place of the law that the first person of the Trinity is dominant at Sinai. The Son himself would, in his life, be subject to this law. 'Think not that I am come to destroy the law, or the prophets: I am not come to destroy, but to fulfil' (Matt. 5:17).

Let us note the way in which the law was given.

Observe in the first place that it was a mountain from which God spoke. A mountain is a symbol of majesty. God is high and lifted up. He is unique in the excellence of his attributes and is glorious in holiness. Who can attain to him? Even if we could scale the mountain we would find that he inhabited eternity beyond the mountain. It is better for us to wait in the valley and hear the commands he gives us and trust in his enabling to fulfil his requirements.

Not a mountain only but a mountain on fire confronted the people. The light and heat drove the people back. They were reminded that God lives in light unapproachable, whom no one has seen nor can see (1 Tim. 6:16).

Yet, mysteriously, the light was accompanied by a blackness and darkness. This may well have been like the three days of darkness that came upon the Egyptians during the time of their judgment, a darkness that could be felt. What are we to understand by this? Those who have come under the condemning power of the law know best what this is.   It is the despair of being judged guilty and deserving of condemnation.   It is the experience of being shut out of all that is worthy.   It is to know and feel the sentence of guilt pronounced.   It is to feel wrath and punishment.   Jude declares that a place of blackest darkness is reserved for the wicked.   The writer to the Hebrews calls it darkness and gloom (Heb. 12:18).

In addition to fire and light, darkness and blackness, there was tempest and earthquake.   These physical events resulted in spiritual experience.   There was a feeling that life's foundations were breaking up.   All security was being removed.   The self-righteous, self-sufficient man says that he will never be moved.   Once exposed to God, however, and especially to the holiness of God, the storm winds begin to blow in man's soul.   The foundations he thought to be secure began to twist and turn and break up under his feet.   The spiritual earthquake and soul-storm is terrible for him.   He is gripped by distress of an intensity formerly unknown.

What of the sound of the trumpet?   This was dreadful too!   It was the inescapable summons to the people to appear and hear the sentences of the law.   It was a summons which could not be resisted.   It was a pledge of future judgment.   When the last trumpet shall sound, all flesh will have to answer to the demands of the law and give account.   Excuses will be useless.   There will be no way of escape.

The sound of the voice of God was such that the people were not able to bear it.   The dreadful visible manifestations were enough to terrify them.   But this speech of God himself they found utterly overwhelming.   This audible voice was majesty and terror at its height.   The ten commandments are the only words which he has spoken to a whole nation and the only words he has inscribed himself on tables of stone.   To a guilty transgressor the words of the law are unbearable.   The carnal mind hates those words, is not subject to them, neither indeed can be (Rom. 8:7).

The total apartness or holiness of God was seen in the fact that if so much as a beast crossed over to touch the mountain it was stoned to death, or shot through with a dart.   The lesson was one in which the people were to understand that they were to keep back.   This killing of the beast showed the heinous and execrable nature of any offence against the holiness of God.   An understanding of this in the heart colours and affects a man's entire religious experience.

We find that Moses himself was not exempt from fear.   He expressed his terror by saying, 'I exceedingly fear and quake' (Heb. 12:21).   If he, who was so eminently privileged and experienced felt that way, where would you and I appear?

If the very words of God in law-giving troubled the people exceedingly, so did the fire. Fire was blazing in the sky (Deut. 4:11) and three times the people mentioned this as a chief cause of their dread (Deut. 5:24-26). Our God is described as a consuming fire (Deut. 4:24; Heb. 12:29). Fire is not the symbol of God's wrath only but the literal means of his executing wrath. Paul says of those who do not obey the Gospel that they 'shall be punished with everlasting destruction and shut out from the presence of the Lord and from the glory of his power; When he shall come to be glorified in his saints' (2 Thess. 1:9,10).

No truth is more unpopular than this and none more subject to neglect. The attention we have given to the moral law should indicate that God's wrath is always the result of justice. The law tells us what sin is. The one who transgresses the commandments is a sinner. The law sentences the sinner to just punishment in which the whole character of an angry and offended God is affected. His attitude and response to any and every form of sin is not only understood in terms of the law given at Sinai, but also in the context of the crucifixion of Christ outside the walls of Jerusalem. It is precisely the same law and justice given by God at Sinai that demanded that Christ should pay the full price. He had to bear the wrath and punishment as our substitute before we could receive forgiveness. Dereliction was the price paid for atonement.

The deeper our understanding and appreciation of the law as it proceeds from God its giver, the better and sounder our whole experience of Christ. If our experience of Sinai is light and superficial then our grasp of and gratitude for the Gospel will be equally shallow.

The law has a vital role to play both before and after conversion. As the Old Testament precedes the New, so does the law precede the Gospel. The setting up of an altar of sacrifice follows the giving of the law. After Jesus has asserted in his ministry that he had not come to abolish the law but to fulfil it – then he became the only sacrifice which propitiates that blazing fire treasured up by God's justice against wretched offenders.

With Christ also came the clearest summary of the moral law: that the Triune God should be loved with all the heart. That includes mind, affections, emotions and will – everything.

Chapter 9

The Experience of Law
before Conversion

JOHN NELSON was one of the band of famous Methodist preachers who travelled the length and breadth of the land during the years of the great Eighteenth-Century Awakening. In writing about his experience, he tells of his convictions which began when he was between nine and ten years old. He experienced such impressions of the world to come at that tender age that it was as though he saw the judgment enacted by direct sight. He saw a stream of souls coming to the bar of judgment, and every one that came compared his conscience with the book and went directly to his place, either singing or else crying and howling. Those that went to the right hand were but like the stream of a small brook whereas the others were like the flowing of a mighty river!

Powerful convictions followed through the years. Nelson made many resolutions but was not converted. In his early twenties he earnestly sought to get right with God, attending all kinds of churches including Quaker and Roman Catholic. Then he heard Whitefield and Wesley, both of whom made profound impressions of deep conviction and hope upon him. Still he was not converted. This eventually came, but enough of John Nelson's testimony has been described to show that there can be potent and numerous convictions and yet no conversion. Jonathan Edwards, too, describes the powerful conviction of which he was the subject before conversion.

Several cases can be cited from Scripture of those who feared God, who experienced a legal conviction of sin, but were never brought to conversion. Pharaoh is one such. He was moved to fear by the lightning, thunder and hail. 'I have sinned this time,' he said. His conviction did not last very long.

Balaam understood much about God and desired the noble blessings given to Israel. Balaam confessed that he was a sinner but did not experience conversion (Num. 22:34; 2 Pet. 2:15). Who would doubt the convictions of Judas? But they were not convictions of repentance; only of fear, guilt and despair.

The difference between legal and evangelical experience is explained well by Edwards:

In a legal humiliation, men are made sensible that they are little and nothing before the great and terrible God, and that they are undone, and wholly insufficient to help themselves; as wicked men will be at the day of Judgment: but they have not an answerable frame of heart, consisting in a disposition to abase themselves, and exalt God alone. This disposition is given only in evangelical humiliation, by overcoming the heart and changing its inclination, by a discovery of God's holy beauty.

When he says they have not an answerable frame of heart to exalt God, he means they lack saving faith. Repentance is to turn from sin and to hate and forsake it, but repentance also involves a change of mind or heart by which the sinner believes in Jesus Christ and is enabled to see Christ's atonement as applied to him personally. In other words, the sinner exalts and praises God for salvation. He admires the wonderful provision of God for his soul.

Edwards continues:

In a legal humiliation, the conscience is convinced, as the consciences of all will be most perfectly at the day of Judgment; but because there is no spiritual understanding, the will is not bowed nor the inclination altered: this is done only in evangelical humiliation. In legal humiliation, men are brought to despair of helping themselves: in evangelical they are brought voluntarily to deny and renounce themselves; in the former, they are subdued and forced to the ground; in the latter they are brought sweetly to yield, and freely and with delight to prostrate themselves at the feet of God.

Here again we observe faith functioning in yielding to God and delighting in his provision.

No conviction of sin

Pathetic is the state of those who believe themselves to be true Christians but who never have experienced any conviction of sin. Many have registered a decision for Christ and been encouraged on that basis to believe that all is well. A counsellor or perhaps a preacher has assured them that they must be saved.

'But, I don't feel saved,' is the retort made!

'Don't go by your feelings,' is the advice given.

Now, while the mind must be persuaded, conversion is not confined to the intellect. The whole man is involved. Feelings are included. To go by feelings alone is just as unbalanced as reckoning only with the mind. The exclusion of feelings or emotions in conversion is ridiculous. A bridegroom does not anticipate marriage without feeling! The Scriptures liken union with Christ by faith to marriage (Rom. 7; Eph. 5). The entire person is involved. That a man feels himself to be a sinner and that he be cut to the heart about his guilt is good. If this drives him to seek forgiveness through Christ it will lead to his salvation.

The testimony of a nineteen-year-old girl will illustrate what is meant by conviction of sin before conversion and also what it is for feelings to be involved.

'I then went to bed and soon after to sleep but I had not slept long before I awoke in very great terror. I thought I was sinking through the bed and that hell was open to receive me. So great was my terror that I was bathed in perspiration and I took hold of my little brother and held him so fast that he screamed aloud with pain. Oh the terrors of that night, I know not how the night got over but it left me in great misery. But I thought I would put it all away. It would be time enough to think about religious matters when I was older and settled in life.' A few months after this, the young lady was truly converted.

Of the struggle associated with repentance or a change of heart many professing Christians know nothing. The Scriptures declare the fear of God to be the beginning of wisdom. Concerning this fear they have not the faintest conception. They have been deceived by false shepherds. They know nothing of true salvation. They are still in their sins. Such people, who think they are true believers, can be a great menace in a church. They maintain a form of godliness but deny the power of it. They are destitute of true soul experience and when faced with these realities turn away.

Often the reality of the fear of God comes to them for the first time by way of the preaching of the doctrines of grace, sometimes referred to as the Reformed Faith.   They hear of man's total depravity, of human inability, of God's right to save whom he wills.   But they abhor and loathe these truths because their whole concept of the Gospel rests on the premise that salvation is merely a matter of man's decision.

Little conviction or much?

To safeguard those who have truly repented but who have experienced a minimum of conviction of sin is important.   It is also very important that this experience of conviction is not stereotyped. For example, in Acts 16 we have two people who experienced salvation in different ways.   Both had repentance and faith.   Both turned from ungodliness and unrighteousness to embrace Jesus Christ.   Lydia saw the loveliness of Christ as Paul preached.   The Lord opened her heart and she embraced him as Lord and Saviour, quietly and sweetly without tempest, earthquake or thunder.   Undoubtedly Lydia had repentance, but faith is uppermost in her experience.   With the Philippian jailor we find a man overwhelmed with conviction.   He cries out in anguish.   His experience is shattering, like the earthquake under him.   Repentance is uppermost and faith must be urged.   'Believe,' cries Paul, 'Believe on the Lord Jesus Christ, and thou shalt be saved.'   It would be wrong, however, to come to the conclusion that the blackest and worst sinners must of necessity be subject to the most intense convictions and be alarmed by the terrors of hell.   The work of grace can be gradual in really profligate sinners.

John Newton, 1725-1807, was awakened to some sense of his dangerous condition before God during a violent and prolonged storm at sea.   He became convinced in his mind that he was the greatest of sinners and doubted whether there could be salvation for him.   But his heart was not moved by very deep feelings or terrors. He later testified: 'It was not till long after (perhaps several years), when I had gained some clear views of the infinite righteousness and grace of Christ Jesus my Lord, that I had a deep and strong apprehension of my state by nature and practice: and perhaps till then I could not have borne the sight. So wonderfully does the Lord proportion the discoveries of sin and grace. For he knows our frame, and that were he to put forward the greatness of his power, a poor sinner would be instantly overwhelmed, and crushed as a moth.' In Newton's case it is clear that grace existed in him for several years to a small degree and then his experience of conviction and of grace grew in intensity. Let it be stressed that we must avoid stereotyping religious experience.

John Bunyan, in his autobiography *Grace Abounding to the Chief of Sinners*, describes his conversion experience. For two years he underwent intense conviction of sin. For instance, one day he sat down beside a roadway, 'and fell into a very deep pause about the most fearful state my sin had brought me to; and, after long musing, I lifted up my head, but me thought I saw as if the sun that shineth in the heavens did grudge to give light, and as if the very stones in the street, and tiles upon the houses, did bend themselves against me; methought that they all combined together to banish me out of the world; I was abhorred of them, and unfit to dwell among them, or be partaker of their benefits, because I had sinned against the Saviour.'

Those who have experienced conviction of sin will understand a description like this, as do pastors who have had to counsel those under such convictions. Simplistic, easy formulas fail completely to remove the burden. Superficial counselling is tantamount to mockery. Relevant passages of Scripture should be expounded and the convicted person urged to seek the Lord, sue for mercy and plead for assurance which it is God's sole prerogative to give.

Those passages of Scripture where the sweet overtures, invitations and offers of mercy are set forth are particularly helpful to those who feel themselves to be so bad that there can be no mercy for them.

The objection may be made that such deep convictions apply only to exceptional people like John Bunyan or C. H. Spurgeon, who likewise went through a prolonged experience of conviction before conversion. But this is not so. Preachers who sustain a doctrinal, expository and systematic ministry today find people subject to this kind of experience. It applies, also, to people of all ages. Convictions vary considerably, some being convicted by one part of the moral law, some by another.

Paul's pre-conversion experience

Paul declares he was convicted by the tenth commandment, and by that brought to an end of all false hopes. He says that he would never have known the sin of his heart if the law had not said, 'you must not covet,' which is the same as saying, 'you must not have evil desires,' or 'do not desire what belongs to someone else' (Rom. 7:7). That commandment came to him and stirred up all manner of evil desires in him.

Paul says he was 'alive without the law once, but when the commandment came, sin revived, and I died'. The law was there all the time but the Holy Spirit began to use it to work upon him saying, 'What about this, then? – and what about that?' A whole world of evil desires latent within him was uncovered. As Robert Haldane puts it, 'the law excited and discovered in him those corruptions of which he had been unconscious.' And then it was as though the evil desires responded by saying, 'Hey! you're not coming to interfere with us are you? We will show you a thing! We will lust harder and more and defy you to do anything about us! We give our master a lot of pleasure and we're not having you messing about with us!'

In this way sin was aroused to activity taking the opportunity to stir up a wide variety of evil desires. Also, it is a fact of fallen human nature that whatever is prohibited is only the more earnestly desired.

In itself the law is absolutely pure. It is only an instrument. It is like a pure silver spoon put into a bowl of horribly rotten meats, stirring up the decay to remind the cook that there is no good in it. The spoon is perfect; the contents of the bowl vile.

Paul was left with no chance of being saved by satisfying the demands of the law. All the law did in that respect was to kill and destroy any aspiration entertained of being saved by his own good works or righteousness. He charged his fellow Jews of ignorantly trying to make themselves good enough for God by the law instead of receiving Christ's righteousness as a gift (Rom. 10:3,4). It must be stressed that this was a vital and essential part of his experience.

Enough has been said to show that conviction of sin before conversion is a factor of immense importance. Anything which negates the rightful place of the moral law in preaching should be shunned. The nature and the role of the law cannot be overestimated in these days when there is so much feeble preaching.

Let us bring back the schoolmaster that we might expect many more applicants who welcome obedience to the Gospel. The law is able to drive men to Christ and cause them to look for, and if possible storm, the very gates of heaven to be sure that they are reconciled to God. Such will never be disappointed and will never be confounded in the great day of reckoning, because they have renounced their self-righteousness and trusted wholly in Christ.

Chapter 10

The Wretched Man of Romans Seven Sorted Out

WE have seen that the law has an essential role before conversion. 'The law was our schoolmaster to bring us unto Christ' (Gal. 3:24). The law was given by Moses to convince the Jews of their transgressions as well as instruct them as to the requirements of God. The law was given to convince men of the necessity of a Saviour. The law exposed their guilt but could afford no remedy for the removal of it. The law is described as a schoolmaster because the Jews were confined under the discipline and fear of it like school-children not permitted to go out at recess.

Since the law did no more than convince them of their lost and undone condition from which they could not escape, they would be more disposed to follow Christ to freedom since he has the full solution for sin and guilt.

Is there no further role for the schoolmaster once we have received forgiveness and justification? The confinement under the school of the law no longer applies. We are made free now, not to break the law but rather to use it as our guide. This distinction is essential.

In the seventh chapter of Romans the apostle sets out the place of the law in the clearest fashion as follows:

1. The law can never justify (7:1-6).
2. The law served to bring Paul under conviction of sin (7:7-13).
3. The role of the law in the believer's experience (7:14-25).

The fourteenth verse of the chapter is the turning point, for there the apostle switches from the past tense to the present tense. He begins at that point to describe what the law did to him as a believer. As he concludes his description he cries out, 'O wretched man that I am!'

Since true religion was never designed to make men miserable, it is felt by some that this description could not possibly apply to Christians or, if it does it is an abnormal experience from which the Christian should try to escape as soon as possible. It is unthinkable, it is said, that believers should go about feeling wretched. They should be rejoicing always because of their justification. Because of statements such as these, the idea has become popular that Romans 7 is a state through which some believers pass, but it is only on the way to the normal state described at the beginning of Romans 8. The sooner the condition of Romans 8 is reached, the better.

In contrast to that, there are others who say that Romans 7 describes the Christian in his very best condition, and that the more mature a believer is the more he appreciates the sentiments of the concluding section of Romans 7 as descriptive of himself.

When difficulties and differences of interpretation such as this arise it is good to stand back and view Romans 7 within the perspective of the whole life of the apostle and all his writings. He certainly never went around as a man lamenting his dreadful calamity and smiting his breast continually saying, 'O wretched man that I am!' However, we can recognise in him a basic and deep humility which colours all his actions and sayings. We can see the principles of Romans 7 at work all the time. Those principles are the perfect requirements of God's law, love for that law, an ever-present awareness of the flesh being unable to satisfy those demands, and a realistic understanding of the limitations and inability of human nature. But at the same time there is an appreciation of the corresponding abilities of the spiritual mind as enabled by the Holy Spirit. Constant awareness of indwelling sin (and the need to mortify it) and of life in the Spirit as portrayed in Romans 8 characterised Paul's testimony. There is surely no need to divorce the one from the other. The experience of human inability and of God's enabling is concurrent. There is absolutely no need to set up a conflict between Romans 7 and 8 and divide them asunder. Indeed it is only the man who knows his weakness that lives by God's strength. God's strength is made perfect in weakness.

We need to go further and recognise the ebb and flow, the ups and downs, in the ocean-tide of Christian experience. Surely, it hardly needs saying that the average Christian has occasions of deep conviction of sin. He does not feel that conviction every moment he lives. Isaiah did not spend the whole of his life experiencing the sight of the Lord's glory in the temple and the conviction of uncleanness that followed. Jonah did not spend the whole of life living inside the fish's belly. There are times when the wretchedness of sin is felt by us. The good work of conviction is done and we go forward. The feeling of it passes away, but not altogether. It is there, ready always to return to fulfil a good work in us by portraying the perfection we must strive to attain and our need of spiritual ability to attain it.

To summarise, we see, firstly, that experience of the wretchedness of the flesh and the power of the Spirit are concurrent – not separated into watertight compartments, but felt and experienced together. Secondly, both these aspects of experience form part of the full ocean of experience. There are many other aspects as the chapter titles suggest and no one experience should be isolated and exalted at the expense of the others.

However, the wretched man of Romans 7 is still not sorted out. Can we be sure that he is indeed a Christian, and not only a Christian but a Christian at the zenith of his experience rather than at an immature level?

To proceed directly then, who but a mature believer of advanced experience holds together at one and the same time very clear views of the various elements which constitute the spiritual warfare of the Christian? Paul brings together the law of God and its demands, an understanding of the nature of the opposition to that law by indwelling sin, and a full view of where our strength lies.

According to Jonathan Edwards, one of the most important signs of regeneration is that a person delights in the holiness or moral excellence of God. That is a very important matter, because it is the opposite of the unregenerate nature. The essence of the unregenerate nature is that it is not subject to the law of God, neither indeed can be. The mark of the regenerate, on the other hand, is that he is subject to God's law. Here we find Paul delighting in the law of God after the inward man (v. 22). The inward man represents the very heart and core of a man, his mind or centre of his personality. If in his inmost being he delights in God's law, that surely can only be the result of renewal. If a man in his will and affections is in love with God and his law, surely that is decisive evidence that he is born from above?

With this mind, Paul served the law of God (v. 25). To please God is what absorbed him. He was intent on fulfilling the spiritual content of the law. Such represents the mind of a regenerate man.

How can the objection be answered that Paul in the same context complains about being carnal and sold under sin and doing what he hated? Did not Elijah say to Ahab, 'Thou hast sold thyself to work evil in the sight of the Lord' (1 Kings 21:20)?   But Paul is not saying that he has abandoned himself to evil, but rather that the indwelling propensity to sin was in and of itself totally evil.   There could be no compromise whatever with indwelling sin which he designates or calls 'the flesh'.   Of that flesh he has nothing good to say.   It is wholly sinful, sold under sin.

Now, the more a man is in love with God and his will as reflected in the moral law and all his precepts, the more sensitive he will be to the contradiction to that law that he still finds within his nature as a man.   The unwillingness to respond, the sloth, the resistance to that which is right – all this is a cause of trouble and grief to a truly spiritual person.   'O how love I thy law! it is my meditation all the day' declares the psalmist (Ps. 119:97).   Intimate acquaintance with the law brings a knowledge of its spiritual content and the full import of its requirements.   Such a knowledge results in painful awareness of shortcoming and deficit in fulfilment of what is required.   Oh yes, we have been forgiven and justified, but how far short we fall of what we desire to be.   Instead of being as swift of foot as was Asahel we find lead weights on our feet.   Our performance is sluggish and wretched.   The cry from our hearts is real, 'O wretched man that I am!'   It is because we know what kind of performance we *should* give that we are so unhappy with what we *do* produce for God.   This is not an exercise in futility.   It is an invaluable reckoning with reality and a coming to grips with the limitations we experience as those who are still in the flesh.   These factors press us to avail ourselves to the full of those resources the Holy Spirit has for us which are described in Romans 8.

A man in his very best spiritual condition recognises the conflict and what it is all about – 'The flesh lusteth against the Spirit, and the Spirit against the flesh: and these are contrary the one to the other: so that ye cannot do the things that ye would' (Gal. 5:17).

The wretched man of Romans 7, then, is not a libertine who says that he couldn't care less about God's law.   He is not antinomian, that is one who disregards the law and falls into all manner of sins because he refuses to heed that which is defined by the law as sin. The wretched man is one who delights in the law as holy, just, good and spiritual.

The wretched man of Romans 7 is not a legalist who is so stupid as to think that he can gain justification by the law.   Nobody knows the first six verses of chapter seven better than the wretched man himself.   After all, the wretched man was the author of the epistle to the Galatians which warns strongly that the law should never be used as a basis for justification.   To him the law is knowledge and instruction.   Christ only is his justification.   Christ who kept the law perfectly for him is his justification.   Christ his righteousness vindicated the law.   Christ who is his justification expounded the law in the sermon on the mount.   Finally, it is Christ who died because of the penalty which the law inflicts upon transgressors.

The wretched man of Romans 7 is Paul the realist who has come to know the nature of the fight, the enemy within and, best of all, the victory that is his through Christ.   For this the wretched man is everlastingly thankful.

The wretched man of Romans 7 not only stands for Paul who wrote it, but represents every Christian who is reckoning realistically with the battle of the flesh as it wars against the Spirit.   The wretched man, dear Christian, is you!   It is you viewed in a particular way. If this is not part of your experience then you still have a long way to go.

God intends that the work of sanctification should form part of our lives. This involves the process of eradicating sin. The law is essential to this end. If a man lives only for his happy experiences he is likely to be a carnal prig. Thinking himself to be blessed, he will be oblivious of the world of sin within which will certainly be observed by others. No man is more wretched than the man who has never discovered his true wretchedness and God's remedy to deal with it.

Chapter 11

Joy because of Justification

WE have seen that humiliation because of sin is the first experience of Christianity and without it there can be no salvation. The good news of the Gospel is for sinners only. The self-righteous cannot be saved because they trust in themselves and their own works. The degree to which sinners will experience conviction and feel their guilt varies. After conversion the experience of humiliation because of sin can be intense as is seen in many examples – Job, Isaiah, Peter and Paul. The depth of humiliation has a profound effect upon the believer, particularly with reference to understanding and practising the doctrines of grace. Spurgeon put it this way:

Hardly a glimmer of the humbling truth of our natural depravity dawns on the dull apprehension of the worldly-wise, though souls taught from above know it and are appalled by it. In divers ways the discovery comes to those whom the Lord ordains to save. . . . There is a vital connection between soul-distress and sound doctrine. Sovereign grace is dear to those who have groaned deeply because they see what grievous sinners they are. Witness Joseph Hart and John Newton whose hymns you have often sung, or David Brainerd and Jonathan Edwards, whose biographies many of you have read.[1]

Also we have observed that the new birth takes place after, before or during conviction, *i.e.* in some cases it might precede, in other cases it might follow. That the new birth precedes saving faith and saving repentance is fundamental to the Reformed faith, but, again as we have seen, it has always been a matter of debate as to how much conviction or preparation goes on in a sinner before the new birth is wrought by the Holy Spirit. Some believe in more preparatory work prior to the new birth than others. Jonathan Edwards in his writings shows that during revivals many come under deep convictions, only to fall away in the course of time. Conviction of sin must be evangelical, that is it must be toward God.

While humiliation for sin plays a dominant and abiding role in the realm of experience, so too does joy. Indeed, the deeper and stronger the roots of humiliation, the greater and better the tree which will be full of the most glorious fruit of joy. Richard Sibbes uses another figure suggesting that,

There are two eyes in experience, one upon God and one upon our present situation. God will bring us to comfort but it must be by a sense of our own unworthiness. He will forgive our sins but it must be by the sight and sense of our sins. He will bring us to life but it must be by death. He will bring us to glory but it must be by shame, God works by contraries: therefore in contraries believe contraries.[2]

The whole life should radiate joy, power, peace and purity in the Holy Ghost (Rom. 14:17), but this cannot be unless there is a clear understanding of what sin is and a commensurate appreciation of the magnitude of God's grace. Paul truly felt and believed himself to be the chief of sinners. His gratitude was unbounded and this was reflected in his worship and service of God. Those who have little, if any, conviction wonder at this. Let us hear Spurgeon again:

I question whether any one coming among us could bear to see himself as God sees him. I think it is highly probable that, if any man were to see his own heart as it really is, he would go mad; it would be a sight too dreadful for an awakened conscience and a sensitive reason to endure. And when the Lord does come to any of his servants, and reveals sin in its true character, unless there is a corresponding revelation of the cleansing blood, it puts man into a very dreadful condition of mind.[3]

We might get to grips with the subject of joy as an experience by using the following headings:

1. What is joy?
2. The joy of salvation
3. Joy because of justification.
4. The relationship of joy to power.
5. How to obtain joy.

1. What is joy?

Joy can be defined as a sense of gladness or delight. It is a quality of heart, a well-being of soul. It can be steady and express itself in the singing to oneself of psalms, hymns and spiritual songs, or it can be intense and unrestrained, expressing itself in the form of leaping for joy. The Hebrew verb *gil gul* means to leap or to have intense joy. The other word, used more frequently in the Old Testament, is *simchah* denoting rejoicing, gladness or mirth. Associated with these words is the idea of excitement.

In the New Testament we again find two words used. *Chara*, which is more frequently found, simply means joy, while *agalliasis* denotes intense joy. This last word is related to the concept of leaping. We read of the lame man at the gate of the temple called Beautiful who, when he was healed, immediately received strength in his feet and ankle bones and, leaping up, entered into the temple, walking and leaping and praising God. To be joyful is to find our souls leaping with praise and gladness. When the ark was brought up to Jerusalem it was by dancing and leaping that David gave expression to the joy of his soul (2 Sam. 6:16).

Joy is an attribute of God. It is customary to think of the attributes of God as communicable and incommunicable; immutability, eternity, infinity, omnipotence and omniscience constituting those attributes of which we do not, and of which we cannot, partake. Among the communicable attributes are: love, justice, anger, holiness, patience and joy. Some of these attributes of which we partake belong to the realm of heart experience.

Rightly we associate joy with life. In getting to grips with the meaning of joy it is helpful to observe the difference between the joy of God and the frustration of the unbelieving world that rejects God. Men long for life, fulfilment, satisfaction. The tragedy is that they are at enmity with God and refuse to look to the only source of fulfilment. They seek joy and cannot find it. The ungodly man is ever in quest of joy and often confuses joy with carnal gratification or sensual pleasure. William Romaine states the matter well when he says:

They are busy, and weary themselves in the pursuit of it, and cannot find it. While they are turned in heart from the Lord, they look downwards for it; where it is not. They expect it will spring out of the ground: and if they cannot discover it upon the surface, they will dig into the bowels of the earth for treasures of hidden joy. But they disquiet themselves in vain. It is the sovereign decree of the Almighty that nothing can make the sinner truly happy but God in Christ.[4]

It would be strange if we did not find joy among the attributes of God, for the three persons of the Trinity in themselves enjoy perfect felicity without the addition of any created beings (Prov. 8:30). The angels rejoiced in the creation (Job 38:7) and God viewed with satisfaction that which he had made (Gen. 1:31). We do not read that he rejoiced over the creation, but he does rejoice and even sing over redemption. He sings over his redeemed people. 'The Lord thy God in the midst of thee is mighty; he will save, he will rejoice over thee with joy; he will rest in his love, he will joy over thee with singing' (Zeph. 3:17).

Likewise, the Father's gift to him of a people is the joy of Christ. For this joy set before him he endured the cross (Heb. 12:2). The joy of salvation is also reflected in Paul's words to the Philippians where he describes them as, 'my joy, and crown' (Phil. 4:1). As the bridegroom rejoices over the bride so does Christ rejoice over his church (Ps. 45:11; Rev. 21:2).

The angels rejoice over one sinner who repents (Luke 15:10), a timely reminder to us that we are to rejoice in the same way. It is a temptation during barren times, when very few are saved, to cease to marvel and rejoice in the salvation of the few that may make up the local church. If we cease to rejoice over our brothers and sisters, then we have in one way lost touch with heaven and eternity, for eternity will be taken up in understanding and extolling the wonders of God's grace in salvation (Eph. 1:1-13).

The very life of God is a life of joy and into that life we are brought by the truth of the Gospel. The life of Christ is a life of joy and to be in union with him is to partake of his joy. Hence he prays that 'they might have my joy fulfilled in themselves' (Jn. 17:13).

The joy of God's people is threefold. i. The joy of salvation. ii. The experience which follows, namely, the joy of communion with the triune God, this being the joy of eternity. (Man's chief end is to glorify God and enjoy him for ever, *Westminster Shorter Catechism*, 1). iii. The joy we derive from the gifts which God gives us. ('How shall he not with him also freely give us all things?' (Rom. 8:32).)

2. *The joy of salvation*

Says Paul: 'We joy in the atonement (reconciliation)' (Rom. 5:11). Unless we have some assurance of having been reconciled to God, true joy is impossible. On the other hand, a strong assurance of reconciliation and of God's love to us helps to assist and increase our joy. Note the experience of John Flavel, and particularly the relationship between Christian joy and 'the full assurance of his interest' in salvation:

There going on his way his thoughts began to swell and rise higher and higher like the waters in Ezekiel's vision, till at last they became an overwhelming flood. Such was the intention of his mind, such the ravishing tastes of heavenly joys, and such the full assurance of his interest therein, that he utterly lost all sight and sense of the world and all the concerns thereof, and for some hours he knew no more where he was than if he had been in a deep sleep upon his bed. Arriving in great exhaustion at a certain spring he sat down and washed, earnestly desiring, if it was God's good pleasure, that this might be his parting place from the world. Death had the most amiable face in his eye that ever he beheld, except the face of Jesus Christ which made it so, and he does not remember, though he believed himself dying, that he even thought of his dear wife and children or any earthly concernment. On reaching his inn the influence still continued banishing sleep – still, still the joy of the Lord overflowed him and he seemed to be an inhabitant of the other world. He many years after called that day one of the days of heaven, and professed that he understood more of the life of heaven by it than by all the books he ever read or discourses he ever entertained about it.[5] (Flavel wrote this in the third person, it being assumed by most readers that he was describing his own experience.)

The joy of salvation can be viewed as continuing and growing in depth through this life, and also as eternal. The Ethiopian eunuch, having had salvation in Christ revealed to him, 'went on his way rejoicing' (Acts 8:39). The Philippian jailor 'rejoiced, believing in God with all his house' (Acts 16:34). This joy of salvation, though fluctuating because of trials and testings, should increase as the believer is grounded and settled in the truth. Joy is also described as 'everlasting'. 'And the ransomed of the Lord shall return, and come to Zion with songs and everlasting joy upon their heads: they shall obtain joy and gladness, and sorrow and sighing shall flee away' (Is. 35:10).

Not all apparent joy is genuine, for in the parable of the sower we are warned of 'stony ground hearers', who receive the word with joy, but not having any root in themselves, endure for a little but when tribulation or persecution arises they fall away (Matt. 13:21, 22). Entertainment evangelism, which predominates in many areas and countries, but particularly in North America, tends to produce temporary faith. Many are impressed by fervour, by crowds, by singing and by eloquence. Although they respond to appeals to decide for Christ they are not savingly joined to Christ and therefore they fall away. Their joy is produced by feelings only rather than by union with Christ by faith.

Joy because of salvation and joy in the God of salvation should always be central and predominant, but this very often is not the case when a teaching ministry and biblical oversight are absent. Some who are not truly converted become active in such churches. Their experience is one which is fed by feelings. A good service to them is a service in which there is emotion, excitement or activity. They are able to discuss external questions about organization and can converse about practical matters and even argue about doctrine at the intellectual level, but when it comes to experience of the heart and communion with God, they are destitute.

3. Joy because of justification

Experience must spring out of salvation and the knowledge of salvation is clarified by the doctrine of justification. Our glorying must be in God's grace and in his free justification of those who believe. This is well illustrated by the case of the seventy disciples who, returning from their preaching mission, rejoiced in the fact of their power over devils. Richard Baxter, commenting on this passage, says:

They relished most delightfully in the external part. But the great end of these miracles they too much overlooked: they left out of their rejoicing the appearances of God, the advantages of faith, the promotion of the spiritual Kingdom of Christ, and the greater mercies of the Gospel as to themselves and others. They took too great a share of the honour to themselves, being more affected to see what great things they were made the instruments to accomplish, than what honour did thereby accrue to God and benefit to man.[6]

Every word of Baxter's statement is applicable today. Is it not true that we all tend by nature to be impressed by externals, by sensations, by the fantastic and fabulous, by statistics, by successes and by glamour stories, whether it be tramping through sweltering jungles, or smuggling Bibles into Communist countries?

Jesus cured what Baxter called the 'diseased joys', and directed the disciples to rejoice in their election, that their names were written in heaven (Luke 10:20). That we are to rejoice in these fundamental blessings of God is very encouraging because it means that we do not have to travel long distances to discover some secret formula for joy. All blessing is near us, even in the Word of God, and the greatest blessings, according to Paul, are election, predestination, adoption, redemption, a knowledge of the truth and of our eternal inheritance (Eph. 1: 1-12). Our experience of joy is connected with all these, but justification underlies them all and supports them all. Our joy should never be apart from the consideration of justification, because justification is based on the atoning death of Christ. Every time we celebrate the Lord's Supper we are reminded of the fact that apart from Christ's sacrifice there is no justification.

Justification vindicates God's holiness, magnifies the doctrines of sovereign grace (Rom. 3:21-26), and provides believers with an impregnable fortress against Satan's wiles and accusations. God the Father justifies believers, and if the Father justifies, who can overthrow such a foundation? (Rom. 8:33-39).

Faith is the means by which we are united to Christ and this union is the basis of our justification. His triumph on the Cross secures our justification and we now see him with the eyes of faith as our saviour and justifier. 'Though we see him not,' says Peter, 'yet believing on him we rejoice with joy unspeakable and full of glory.'

John Brown, in his *Expository Discourses on First Peter*, takes 'ye do rejoice with joy unspeakable' in the future tense, as do a minority of commentators. Brown interprets Peter as contrasting the present trials with the joy of future glory. I believe this interpretation to be erroneous because we have three verbs in the present tense: 'you continue to rejoice' (v. 6), 'you continue to love' (v. 8), 'you continue to rejoice' (v. 8). The present tense verbs for 'you continue to rejoice' are identical in verses 6 and 8. In other words, Peter is speaking of the experience of joy we have now in this present world.

Clear views of justification foster a strong sense of joy because the believer sees his salvation is determined by an omnipotent God. He dare not turn away for he knows that only those who persevere prove to be the elect.   The justified are saved by faith and they live thereafter by faith (Rom. 1:17).   The omnipotent God saves them and they rejoice in such a God who will keep them by his power through faith unto salvation (1 Pet. 1:5).   Richard Baxter states the matter well:

What should be rejoiced in, if not the Lord of life himself who is the everlasting joy and glory of the saints? – other things may be the means of conveyance, but God is the matter of our joy – It is congruous that we now rejoice in that which we must everlastingly rejoice in.   Herein is the state of everlasting joy, and therefore the foresight of it by faith is the only way to rational, solid comfort here.[7]

4. The relationship of joy to power

We have seen that conviction of sin and repentance are essential. Chastisement afterwards results in the peaceable fruits of righteousness (Heb. 12:11).   'Weeping may endure for a night, but joy cometh in the morning' (Ps. 30:5).   The Corinthians were buffeted by controversy over the discipline of the unrepentant, immoral man, but the purging effects were profitable (2 Cor. 7:9-11).   A proper balance must always be observed between what we are and what we deserve as sinners on the one hand and the wonder of justification on the other.   Hence Nehemiah exhorts the people to be joyful – not sorry only, but to be glad, for 'the joy of the Lord is your strength' (Neh. 8:10).

There is power in a rightly-grounded joy.   Paul and Silas, although scourged, sang at midnight though their position in stocks in a dungeon seemed hopeless.   There is something irresistible about a man who has the joy of the Holy Spirit.   He cannot be overcome because by faith he sees Christ, rejoices in Christ, is empowered by Christ and finds that Christ's strength in him is able to overcome opposition from the world.   Note the testimony of Rowland Taylor on his way to martyrdom.   'All the way Taylor was *joyful* and *happy*, as one that accounted himself going to a most pleasant banquet, or bridal feast.   He spake many notable things to the sheriff and yeoman of the guard that conducted him, and often moved them to weep through his earnest calling upon them to repent, and to amend their evil and wicked living. Often, also, he caused them to wonder and rejoice, to see him so constant and steadfast, void of all fear, *joyful in heart and glad to die*' (italics mine).

A joyful believer is a man bold in his witness to Jesus Christ. To be filled with the Holy Spirit is to be filled with the life of God, which means that various characteristics will be observable in a symmetry, balance and proportion; attributes such as meekness, love, wisdom, submission to the truth and the rule of Christ, peace, patience, self-control and joy. All are present but one can predominate at certain times. 'The disciples were filled with joy, and with the Holy Ghost' (Acts 13:52).

Joy imparted by the Holy Spirit through the Word enables men to endure and persevere through difficult times and circumstances as did Jeremiah who testified that God's Word was the joy and rejoicing of his heart (Jer. 15:16). Likewise Habakkuk was sustained in very barren times saying, 'I will rejoice in the Lord, I will joy in the God of my salvation' (Hab. 3:18). Joy will not only strengthen a man to persevere but will help to empower a preacher. John the Baptist declared his joy to be in the Bridegroom, rejoicing greatly because of the bridegroom's voice: 'this my joy therefore is fulfilled' (John 3:29). The Holy Spirit used the advent of Christ to inspire John to be the powerful and influential preacher that he was.

5. *How to obtain joy*

While it is unfortunate that name tags have to be used, it is increasingly evident that two movements in particular claim to have the answers to the needs of believers of the world today, the Reformed and the Charismatic. The Reformed concentrates on truth and the Charismatic on experience. According to the Charismatics, the pathway to joy and power is through an experience called the baptism of the Spirit. Fervent attempts are made to induce this experience. Expressions such as 'Amen Lord' are repeated, choruses are sung, everybody prays at the same time, hands are laid on seekers and some speak in tongues. (This by no means applies to all Pentecostals but does characterize the present Charismatic surge.) Bodily sensations will be felt by seekers akin to the physical impulses felt when hearing music of a most inspired character. In the quest for experience, feeling and emotion is maximised and truth minimised. Experience is sought within the atmosphere of experience and within the context of the experience of others. When it comes to explaining or defining these experiences as they relate to truth we find great difficulty. What produced the experience? Those who have the experience will testify to more love for the Lord and joy. But the experience is mystical and beyond definition. It is subjective inasmuch as it has its seat or location within the person and belongs essentially to feelings. It is not objective as was Stephen's joy in dying when he saw the Lord. Stephen's joy proceeded from Christ to his heart by the Holy Spirit. Stephen's experience was grounded in, and sprang from, the Word, as can be seen from the character of his sermon.

The joy that has its source in feelings alone is transient. This can be illustrated by reference to people who have an intense love for hymns or religious music. By using records or tapes of hymns such people can easily experience joy, but this joy is attached to and belongs to the sentiments of the tunes and the music. Let a crisis or setback suddenly arise and the joy evaporates. In contrast we find the joy which is grounded in the truth will be responsive to setbacks and difficulties. Some can experience joy because they are affected by dramatic architecture and feel a glow within when influenced by certain spatial effects, but remove the buildings and the joy is soon gone. Again, there can be joy when there is exciting activity but when the excitement ends, little joy remains.

The way to obtain joy is to maximise truth but never at the expense of affections, emotions and feelings. Truth is for the whole man. Intellectualism, or truth apart from its application by the Holy Spirit to the whole man, will lead to frigid barrenness. Some have felt themselves to be in the freezing conditions of an arctic, spiritual wilderness, because everything is academic. Hence they have been susceptible to neo-experimentalism as a welcome change.

The way to obtain joy is always through the Scriptures, for the Scriptures alone set forth our union by faith with the Trinity. Union means fellowship with the Trinity and in the experience of this communion there is intense joy. 'These things write I unto you,' says John, 'that your joy might be full.' As we study the writings of the apostles, the truth of our salvation becomes clear and applicable to ourselves and others. In sharing the experience of this truth with others we have joy.

In the Gospel of John we find the subject of joy mentioned only once in the early chapters (John 3:29). However, in the discourses just prior to the crucifixion, our Lord speaks of the subject of joy over and over again. His concern is that his people should have true joy. He did not say to them, 'Let us work ourselves up into an emotional state.' Rather, he set clearly before them the truths which would be the foundation of their joy. The following practical means can be followed to obtain joy.

(i) Seek Joy by continuing in Christ's Love

Let us note again the instruction given in the upper room. 'If ye keep my commandments, ye shall abide in my love; even as I have kept my Father's commandment, and abide in his love. These things have I spoken unto you, that my joy might remain in you, and that your joy might be full' (John 15:10,11).

If you are to have true joy, it is fundamental that you keep the commandments. These commandments, of course, embrace all the precepts and sayings of Jesus – self-denial, loving one another, continuing in his word, etc. By walking in obedience before the Father you will experience his complacent love (John 14:23). By keeping the precepts of our Lord you will likewise abide in his love. Our Lord reminds us of these basic facts 'that your joy might be full'. But what does he mean by 'that my joy might remain in you'? Leon Morris, in his commentary on John, suggests that this joy is the joy of a finished work and is the joy of an inexhaustible power of fresh creation. Godet says that 'my joy' refers to a joy which our Lord himself feels in being the object of the Father's love. John Brown, in his commentary on the discourses of our Lord, seems to have the root of the matter when he says, 'The original words equally admit of the rendering "that my joy in you might remain", as, "that my joy remain in you", and from the very form of expression, "my joy", and "your joy", there seems no reasonable doubt that our Lord announces two separate objects as the ends contemplated by him in his preceding statements and exhortations – that his joy in them might remain, and that their joy in him might abound; and that there are thus two closely connected, but still distinct, motives suggested by him, to wit, that by complying with his command they would minister to his enjoyment, and that by complying with his command they would advance their own happiness.'[8]

(ii) Seek Joy as you read, meditate and pray in private

Very often when we commence a time of devotion we feel empty and dry. The way to joy is not to jump into a pool of our own making, that is a pool of worked-up emotion. Rather the way to joy is through meditation on the truth.

The very fact that we have the Scriptures is a source of joy. 'I have rejoiced in the way of thy testimonies, as much as in all riches' (Ps. 119:14) and, 'I rejoice at thy word, as one that findeth great spoil' (Ps. 119:162). If we are to see the glory of God it will not be apart from the Word since the assurance of our salvation as it comes from this glorious God is revealed in Scripture alone. 'I will greatly rejoice in the Lord, my soul shall be joyful in my God; for he hath clothed me with the garments of salvation, he hath covered me with the robe of righteousness as a bridegroom decketh himself with ornaments, and as a bride adorneth herself with jewels' (Is. 61:10). Such passages as this remind us of the fact that it is the doctrine of justification that seals, settles and clarifies our salvation. Herein we have great joy. If the omnipotent One, who is holy and just, declares us to be righteous that is cause for joy indeed.

(iii) Seek Joy in the corporate worship of the Church

When David was cut off in the wilderness and separated from the sanctuary he recalled the place of worship as the place of great joy. 'I went with them to the house of God, with the voice of joy and praise, with a multitude that kept holyday' (Ps. 42:4). The power and glory of God's presence is promised to those who faithfully gather according to the prescribed worship of the sanctuary. 'The Lord loveth the gates of Zion more than all the dwellings of Jacob' (Ps. 87:2). We can fully expect to experience the joy of the Lord in private and in our family worship, but much more are we to expect this joy as we worship together with God's people.

If, as the apostle Paul points out, it is a personal duty to rejoice always (Phil. 4:4) – how much more is it our duty to seek to regain the true joy of worship and attain that position where we sincerely regard the Lord's day as a delight (Is. 58:13).

If much has to be done to regain personal joy, much more the joy of corporate worship. How blessed will it be when God fulfils his promise to 'make them joyful in my house of prayer' (Is. 56:7). How happy when we can sing the following as a reality:

> *Today on weary nations*
> *The heavenly manna falls,*
> *To holy convocations*
> *The silver trumpet calls,*
> *Where Gospel light is glowing*
> *With pure and radiant beams,*
> *And living water flowing*
> *With soul refreshing streams.*

(iv) Seek Joy in the fellowship of God's people

In his second and third letters, the apostle John speaks of the great joy which he had in knowing that his children walked in the truth. 'I have no greater joy than to hear that my children walk in truth' (3 John 4). We can imagine the apostle's great happiness in hearing, either by letter or by messenger, of the spiritual well-being of those whom he dearly loved in the truth. This joy indicates the warmth and bond of fellowship that existed among the early disciples. To communicate by way of correspondence was a help to joy, but much greater was the joy of face-to-face communion. 'Having many things to write unto you, I would not write with paper and ink: but I trust to come unto you, and speak face to face, that our joy may be full' (2 John 12).

The reason why joy may be lacking among us today is that there is a lack of spiritual content in our conversation and fellowship. We have knowledge and experience to share which far transcend the knowledge of the world. J. W. Alexander wrote as follows: 'Think you any sensual pleasure ever equalled that of Archimedes when he hung over the theorem from which only death could tear him; or of Franklin, when he touched the pendant key, and gave the spark which opened a new world to science? Who can picture the transport of early philosophers, or enquiring Jews, when they first welcomed Christian revelations? The truths that are commonplace to us, were to them the very lights of heaven.'[9] We have so much to share, but negligence so often deprives us of the joy of true spiritual communion with other believers.

These suggestions have been made by which we may obtain joy, but it is good to remember that the Holy Spirit is a person and not a machine. We are not to expect results as we would with mechanical appliances which respond to the pressing of buttons and the turning of switches. The Holy Spirit alone imparts true joy as he reveals the truth to us. In his infinite wisdom and knowledge he sovereignly bestows joy in his own time and way. Nevertheless, it is our responsibility always to seek joy, as John Howe well asserts it: 'Settle this persuasion in your hearts, that the serious, rational, regular, seasonable exercise of delight and joy is a matter of duty, to be charged upon conscience, from the authority of God and is an integral part in the religion of Christians.'[10]

May the joy of the Lord, which is our strength, increasingly be experienced among us and be evident in our churches.

NOTES

1 *The Early Years*, p. 52.
2 Quoted from the 1962 Puritan Conference Papers, p. 26.
3 Sermons, vol. 40, p. 134.
4 *The Life of Faith.*   William Romaine, Works vol. I.
5 Quoted from the 1961 Puritan Conference Papers, p. 58.
6 Quoted from the 1962 Puritan Conference Papers, p. 28.
7 ibid, p. 29.
8 *Discourses and Sayings of our Lord.*   John Brown, vol. 3, p. 292.
9 *Consolation* 1862.   J. W. Alexander, p. 137.
10 Quoted from the 1962 Puritan Conference Papers, p. 28.

Chapter 12

The Experience of Love in Adoption

IN our experience of the love of God we are initiated into what is to be our never-ending experience of the Triune God, the Father in adoption, Christ in union and the love of the Holy Spirit as indweller. The mind is not left out of these rich relationships, but rather it is through the understanding of the mind that the experience of these relationships develops (Rom. 12:1,2). We are not dealing with something mystical in the sense of being indefinable. The Lord Jesus Christ died to redeem us and in the accomplishment of that he himself has joy in reconciling us to the Father and bringing us into a relationship of sonship by adoption. This work is something which we understand and experience. The experience of the love of the Holy Spirit (Rom. 15:30) is seen in what he does for us and in us, a subject expounded to some extent in the chapter on the baptism of the Spirit. Our experience of the love of Christ is contemplated in the final chapter of this book. Here we are to explore the rich experience of the love of God as exemplified in the grace of adoption. There are four main headings under which we shall consider this glorious subject.

1. *Adoption is the ultimate experience*

We were visited by a university student some years ago who was, and still is, characterised by a passion to be sure that he does not miss the mark as a Christian. Above everything else in this wide world of danger and disappointment he wants to be as sure as it is humanly possible to be sure that he has got 'it'. I can say without exaggeration that he has asked me more than a hundred times, 'Pastor, is this it?' 'Yes,' I reply, 'if you have Christ you have "it".' 'Without doubt you have reality because John says that if you have the Son you have life' (I John 5:12). Union with Christ is crucial. If we have union with him we have union with the Father and with the Spirit.

The reasons lying behind our being brought into union with Christ are described in 'the free grace experience' where I have used such superlatives that readers will wonder if there are any left. It ought to be borne in mind however that there is a close connection between the free grace experience and that of being placed into the Christian family by adoption. In the case of free grace it is a matter of probing into the reasons why and finding none but sovereign mercy. Free grace experience is what we feel when we discover that salvation is of God from first to last. Adoption refers to our relationship to the Father and to a way of life that results from that relationship. Free grace is an exercise in worship and thankfulness. Adoption is a way of life before the Father. Free grace is the source, the dynamic and the power in God himself, irresistibly disposing him to save us from our deservings, while adoption is the permanent state to which we are brought. But adoption must not be interpreted as a mere legal state involving a passive experience on our part. Adoption is a legal state but it by no means stops there. Adoption involves active love on our Father's behalf and active reciprocation on ours.

The 1689 Confession of Faith transposed into modern English defines adoption as a grace, 'by means of which they (justified persons) are numbered with, and enjoy the liberties and privileges of the children of God'.

Justification has to do with the law and with God as judge. Justification is the declaration that we are free and totally absolved by the one who has final authority.

Let us picture it this way. The great trial has just ended. When we were found to be guilty of innumerable crimes one stood in our place and satisfied justice on our behalf. The acquitted stands on the steps of the courtroom. He marvels at his justification. Where does he go now? He knows of an abandoned hut on a farm out in the country. Perhaps he can live there and try to find employment in the locality. He does not deserve anything. As an ex-criminal he cannot expect anything.   Just as he is thinking about the hut and a way to live, he is approached by high officials of the great King who tell him that his rooms are awaiting him at the palace where plans have been made for him to live as one of the King's family.   The acquitted has hardly had time to digest the fact of his freedom.   How can this be?   The officials show him the papers which reveal that his new Father knows all about his record and has determined in spite of it to add family rights and an inheritance to the acquittal he has already received.

A place has been prepared and a way of life which will be congenial.   It will be a life based upon a restored relationship, one which is not restored only, but which is rich and full beyond measure.

Looking at all this in perspective we could never underestimate the price paid for the justification of the wretched sinner.   The price paid was enormous—beyond computation.   It brought the condemned to be free, but free only inasmuch as he was standing without condemnation at the top of the steps of the great courtroom.

Without adoption he would have no sure place of residence, no home, no parents, no brothers and sisters.   Adoption brings the prisoner home.   It is true that justification gives him a new coat to wear in place of his former rags, but adoption provides the mansion house to live in with a new family, with the Father as the head, and Christ as the King.

Adoption is the ultimate experience because it is the ultimate of God's purpose for us.   It is the final experience in the sense that it is never ending.   It is the permanent experience or way of life which our Lord procured for us at so great a cost.

2. *Adoption is an experience into which Christ brings us*

Himself God's unique Son by eternal generation, who has always been beside the Father and fully known the Father, Christ came into this world with the specific intention of establishing our adoption.   This objective is seen in his prayer when he prays that those whom the Father has given him may be with him where he is (John 17:24).   This is accomplished through union with him. Through that union believers are not only made holy but are brought into the family. The whole procedure is well portrayed by the writer of the Hebrews letter.

> Both the one who makes men holy and those who are made holy are of the same family. So Jesus is not ashamed to call them brothers. He says,
>> 'I will declare your name to my brothers; in the presence of the congregation I will sing your praises.'
> And again,
>> 'I will put my trust in him.'
> And again he says,
>> 'Here am I, and the children God has given me' (Heb. 2:12,13, NIV).

The picture is one of accomplished redemption in which Christ is found among those who have been made brothers by him.

The joy set before Christ was this family brought by him into sonship. For this prize he endured the cross. In his resurrection he became the firstborn member of the family. He is not only the head of it but the first one to have a glorified human body. All his redeemed brothers will have the same.

Having purchased the family, Christ's concern is to teach all the members how to live in right relationship to the Father. He shows how we should think of the Christian life in terms of adoption. That is the theme of the Sermon on the Mount. That exposition is not a creed for the unbelieving world. It is mainly a description of how Christians should live as sons and daughters by adoption.

Having outlined the character of the Christian in the beatitudes he declares that the function of the believer is to glorify the Father (Matt. 5:16) whose laws must be kept from the heart (Matt. 5:17-48). The aim of every family member is to be like the Father who loves his enemies and who does them good sending them rain, warm sun and full harvests. Our purpose is to be like our Father. We have been born into his family.

In order to achieve this lofty objective our Lord goes on to explain that his brothers must be scrupulous about their motives. Their objective is not to please men. Hence when they give they must not draw attention to their generosity by inviting the attention and praise of men. It is enough that with a single eye they please the Father (Matt. 6:4). Likewise in prayer. The object is not to show others that they are pious. Prayer is to the Father and to assist such prayer the way of approach is given by way of a guide. It is our Father in heaven who is to be worshipped, whose will we must obey, whose daily provision we must look for, whose forgiveness we must plead, whose protection and care we must depend upon.

Our religion must not be with sombre faces to conform to the niggling legalistic notions of others. Our concern is only to please our Father who discerns our motives and knows our hearts. Our concern must not be for the applause of men but for the reward of our Father whose providence we must learn to trust under all circumstances and in all conditions.

The term 'providence' expresses well the special care that pertains because of our adoption into the family. Therefore stress is laid upon the fact that we must not be fretful about clothing and food and how all the bills are to be paid. We are to fulfil our duties and thereafter trust in our Father. As the confession expresses it we 'are pitied, protected, provided for, and chastened by God as by a Father who will never cast us off'. If he clothes the grass of the field will he not clothe us who are his children bought at such a cost. If 'he did not spare his own Son, but gave him up for us all—how will he not also, along with him, graciously give us all things?' (Rom. 8:31, NIV).

Christ's sermon of instruction can be summed up by the exhortation, 'be perfect, therefore, as your heavenly Father is perfect'.

We have seen the Lord's concern to teach his disciples about how to live before the Father. We see also his concern for them to experience the Father's love in adoption. He concludes his prayer in John seventeen by summing up his teaching ministry and confirming this desire for his brothers to experience the Father's love, 'I have revealed you to them, and will continue to make you known in order that the love you have for me may be theirs and I myself may be in them' (John 17:26, NIV).

Since believers are united to Christ it follows that the love with which he has been loved should be experienced by those in union with him. The love that the Father had for the Son is expressed in his earthly ministry. This love was expressed in entrusting him with the responsibility and giving him power and dominion. 'For the Father loves the Son and shows him all he does,' 'the Father has entrusted all judgment to the Son' (John 5:20-22, NIV). 'The Father loves the Son and has placed everything in his hands' (John 3:35, NIV). Similarly those who are united to Christ and loved by the Father are entrusted with responsibility. In receiving Christ we receive the right, authority and power to become the children of the Father—children who have been born from above (John 1:12,13). In loving obedience to the one to whom we are united by faith we obey his teachings and in so doing we experience the Father's love. The obedience is filial—the obedience of sons and the love experienced as a consequence is the love of adoption, or the love that applies to a home and family. 'If anyone loves me, he will obey my teaching. My Father will love him, and we will come to him and make our home with him' (John 14:23).

In this entire experience of life as sons we experience the Father's love which is shed abroad in our hearts by the Holy Spirit. There is unveiled to us in the process the wonder of this love as we come to understand the magnitude of the provision made by the Father for us which leads us to our next consideration.

3. *Adoption represents the full experience of the Father's love*

If the love of Christ and the adoption experience into which he brings us is revealed most fully in John's Gospel, then the love of the Father in that adoption to which we have been brought by Christ is unfolded in Romans, particularly in the fifth and eighth chapters.

Having explained what justification by faith is, Paul describes the fruits of that justification in chapter five. Peace with the Father is one fruit, access to pray is another. Joy is a further fruit, even joy in tribulation, while knowledge of the Father's purpose is yet another. His purpose is that we should learn patience which means stedfastness, which in turn results in experience. This in the context means approvedness. Approvedness confirms our hope and confirms the assurance of the Father's love for us which love is shed abroad in our hearts by the Holy Spirit who is given to us.

All these fruits or blessings are the consequence of the Father's love. It is a love of adoption. All the blessings we receive are based upon the terms of our having been brought by adoption into the intimate family circle.

The phrase 'the love of God is shed abroad in our hearts' is particularly expressive of the experience of adoption. The words 'shed abroad' emphasise the fullness and power of the Father's unchangeable love in the heart which Prof. Murray in his commentary on Romans 5:5 describes as 'the determining centre of thought and life'. What we experience in our hearts is confirmed by the Father's daily care for us.

In Romans eight the apostle turns to this theme of the Father's loving care. He shows love to be the source or fountainhead of all our blessings. All things work together for good for them that love God, who are the called according to his purpose. What is the Father's purpose and why does he control all things for the good of the individuals who have been adopted into his family? His purpose is outlined in what has popularly been called the golden chain which in itself explains why he works all things for the good of those who love him. An analysis of the five points of the golden chain reveals that adoption has its genesis in the Father's unchangeable love. This love has determined that those so loved would be formed into a family perfectly able to enjoy the liberties and privileges of sons.

The word foreknow (them whom he *foreknew*), has led some to think that the term means merely to know beforehand. It includes that, but the way in which it is used in Scripture shows that it means to love in a very special way. For instance in the same epistle it says 'God shall not cast away his people which he foreknew' (Rom. 11:2). The term 'foreknew' conveys the concept of distinguishing love, a love of delight. Many Scriptures show this to be the case (Gen. 18:19, Exod. 2:25, Ps. 1:6, Jer. 1:5, Amos 3:2, John 10:14, 1 Cor. 8:3, 2 Tim. 2:19). Those foreknown are loved with an electing love. The Good News Bible states it simply 'Those whom God had already chosen he also set apart' (Rom. 8:29).

It is this love which we actually experience in the outworking of the love purpose described in the golden chain. We experience this love in the irresistible and omnipotent calling of the Father as he draws us out of the cesspool of a sinful, depraved and ungodly life and separates us to himself. A struggle is involved. We kick against the pricks. It is a matter of grace and love combining to overcome every difficulty. It is God saying, 'Yea, I have loved thee with an everlasting love: therefore with lovingkindness have I drawn thee' (Jer. 31:3).

We can discover no reason why we should receive such love just as we can find no reason why we should receive such grace which fully pardons all and which even overcomes the sin and resistance of unbelief. 'The Lord did not set his love upon you, nor choose you because ye were more in number than any people; for ye were the fewest of all people; but because the Lord loved thee' (Deut. 7: 7,8).

Viewed from above, the Father's action in drawing us and bringing us effectively out of the quagmire of sin, setting us apart, and giving us to Christ is termed 'calling'. Viewed from our end, the receiving end, it is termed conversion. We have seen from our study of conversion how profound this experience can be, not only in the individual but in a church where this almighty power, love and grace are displayed by God.

The love with which we have been loved is such that it provides all that is needed. No detail is overlooked. No event is by-passed. Those who are foreknown are predestinated to be conformed to the image of Christ. Predestination is all embracing. Daily we experience the Father's love. This is the essence of our adoption. Through this we have the comfort of knowing that all the hard things that happen, all the sorrows, heartaches, spiritual agonies and conflicts, can be traced to our Father's love, our Father's provision and our Father's control.

Predestination rightly understood brings us to experience God's affection every day, and brings us to admire his love. We are glad when we can find expressions which describe what we find it hard to express:

> Could we with ink the ocean fill,
> and were the skies of parchment made,
> Were every stalk on earth a quill
> and every man a scribe by trade,
> To write the love of God on high
> would drain the ocean dry,
> Nor could the scroll contain the whole
> though stretched from sky to sky.

The justification obtained for us forms part of the Father's loving provision. Justification by faith being Paul's theme in Romans as a whole, we should not be surprised that he majors on the aspect when he comes to apply these truths in Romans eight. Justification is like the rock of Gibraltar. Justification is the immovable foundation. Nothing can pluck us from the Father's hand once we occupy that position in which he has justified us.

We go on from there to know that because God had made us his sons he will glorify us. We shall be changed. We shall be glorified. Glorification is the consummation of our Father's love and our Father's provision.

Way back in eternity the source of our redemption was our Father's love. The ultimate experience of that is realized in the future glory when as sons and daughters we enjoy our relationship of adoption. Then love will reign. Faith will have given way to sight. Hindrances will be no more. The last tear will have been shed. All things will be new. Adoption will then be known by us as the full experience of the Father's love.

Adoption is a church, or shared experience

The deep concern of our Lord for his family and the way in which they should live together in harmony is expressed sublimely in his high priestly prayer. He prays for the unity of the entire family of believers (John 17:20-26). So impressive is this unity to be that it is to become a foremost factor in evangelism. He prays that we all might be one that the world might believe that he is the sent One. Not only so, but through the beautiful unity of the Church, the outside world is to come into a knowledge of such deep truth as understanding that the believers are loved by God and that Christ is the beloved of the Father (John 17:23).

How, we ask, can such exalted desires find fulfilment in practice? How can a hostile world ever come to see that this strange, religious, isolated group of people called Christians, has a quality of life and a family unity which is of such a standard that it proves the Gospel to be true, and that the Christ is God's sent salvation to the world? In our contemporary world we find that there is very little meaningful contact between believers and unbelievers. It is true that such are thrown together in situations of secular employment, but apart from that it seems there is very little opportunity for the outside world to see the life of spiritual churches. We are reminded by way of illustration of the viewing platforms provided for the public by building contractors in action as they erect office blocks in our cities. People are often fascinated as they stand and watch the preparation of foundations, the setting of steel reinforcing and the pouring of innumerable tons of concrete. From these viewing platforms the public can watch the activity of the builders and follow progress for themselves.

The Christian churches need to provide viewing platforms. This can be done by way of hospitality in the homes and by organising occasions when outsiders can be invited to social functions such as dinner parties where they can meet and get to know the Christians. Our Lord accepted invitations to dinner parties, even from those critical of him such as Simon the Pharisee. There is nothing wrong in dinner parties!

What has all this to do with spiritual experience? My answer is that this has a great deal to do with experience. As Christians, we do live together as a spiritual family and we share together the responsibility to maintain the immensely high standard of unity prayed for by Christ, and explained by, and insisted upon by Paul (Eph. 4:1-6). We share together as part of our spiritual experience the joys and disappointments involved in the growth of the local church. I do not believe our Lord was talking about praying for a formal kind of organized unity established by ecclesiastical dignitaries who confer in the World Council of Churches. The unity prayed for is not one established by speeches and piles of irrelevant papers but one that is seen by our neighbours. True unity belongs to the sphere of constant personal contact in any society. It is not the letter writing I may have with members of the Christian family in other parts of the country or abroad, edifying though that may be. The only unity my neighbours see is that exemplified by Christians living visibly before them in the area and in the community. It is not the ecclesiastical fancy dress parades they may see on television. What personal contact has a viewer with some mitred, brightly decorated archbishop hundreds or thousands of miles away?

When unbelieving people in any given locality begin to see the life of the church in action and start to respond, this becomes a family event. The body becomes very much alive to the possibility of further members being born into it. The situation is similar to pregnancy and birth in family life. Is that not very much an experience for everyone involved in the intimate family? Of course it is!

While we have the idea of a family in mind, reference can be made to the fundamental priority of family unity. Divorce of husband and wife is a tragedy for both which also has disastrous consequences for the children. There are adverse and discouraging effects for all the other relatives as well. The local church is a family in which discipline must be maintained. As problems and difficulties of all kinds are faced and overcome, the family is knitted more closely together. The bond of unity, the mutual love and concern increase as the years go by. The spiritual births in a church, the growing pains and crises passed through—all these make up experience which according to Malachi the prophet will never be forgotten (Mal. 3:16). The translation of church members to be with Christ affects the family very much indeed, whether it be young Stephens at the height of their usefulness or Dorcases of more advanced years.

The adoption of individuals into God's family can be considered on a 'one by one' basis. It is however a major mistake to stop there. This truth has to do with the family. If we separate the doctrine of salvation from the doctrine of the church we can end up as theorists who can talk about knowing God as a science but who lack the reality of spiritual experience as it is related to the church family. Those who neglect the practical issues of church member- ship and submitting to church oversight and correction (Heb. 13: 17) are denying the practical outworking of the experience of adoption. The very word 'church' (1 Cor. 1:1,2) reminds us that adoption is a relationship which we are called into and which we share together (1 John 3:1,2). We experience adoption here on earth *together*, before we experience it *together* in the next life. More- over correction and chastisement form a fundamental and essential part of adoption (Heb. 12:5,6).

The rule of life in our experience together of the Father's adoption is *love*. The new commandment is a commandment of love, to love one another with the same quality of love that Christ shows us (John 13:34). This exalted rule is reinforced by the New Testa- ment letters. Peter insists that *above all* we love one another with a pure heart fervently (1 Pet. 4:8). Paul uses well known analogies to illustrate the bond of union and love and care that must exist. As the human body consists of a variety of members joined indis- solubly into one harmony, likewise members of the church are united together. As a building is made up of stones cemented together so are members of Christ's church cemented into the closest spiritual relationships in a church (1 Cor. 12:12-27, Eph. 2:21,22).

John declares that when believers love one another it is a sure sign that they have passed from death to life. This love is not love at a distance but love exercised under strains and trials. That is what family love is all about. When individual members in trials and difficulties can rely on the affection and practical support of the other members then that is love indeed.

Differences of colour, class, race, upbringing, background, culture, Christian teaching, temperament, personality, aggravations because of ambition or aggressiveness, aggravations caused by the annoying habits or foibles of others, differences of income and standard of living, clashes of political opinion—resentments or 'hang-ups' about maltreatment or lack of appreciation in the past—any of these, or a combination of them, can disrupt unity and cause division in a church. Unity and love that results from being all one in Christ must be a very potent and pervasive spiritual experience if so many problems and differences are going to be overcome and kept in proper perspective.

New Testament teaching on the binding nature of church membership is a reminder of the responsibility that every believer bears in maintaining the unity of the family into which he has been adopted. Added to this some of the most powerful exhortations of the New Testament relate to this matter. This is readily understandable when we remember the necessity of unity. Not only is disunity a travesty of the experience of adoption which we share together but disunity effectively destroys the witness and evangelism of a church. A house divided against itself cannot stand! Inhabitants of any locality will conclude that Christianity is worthless if they see believers wrangling and squabbling among themselves. If the townsfolk attend the worship service of the church and see expressions of division which they might expect to find at a political rally, they are likely to conclude that the religion of these people is sham and humbug. They teach that they are all one brothers and sisters in one united family yet fight and squabble like all the rest! We can understand then why the New Testament takes such a firm line against those who cause division (Rom. 16:17). Also we can appreciate why pleas for unity are so earnest. 'Get rid of all bitterness, rage and anger, brawling and slander, along with every form of malice. Be kind and compassionate to one another, forgiving each other, just as in Christ, God forgave you' (Eph. 4:32, NIV).

The pre-eminent brother in the family has taught us in his model prayer that we can only expect forgiveness from our Father who has adopted us, as we forgive fellow members of the same family (Matt. 5:12). Paul puts it another way when he says, 'Therefore, as God's chosen people, holy and dearly loved, clothe yourselves with compassion, kindness, humility, gentleness and patience. Bear with one another and forgive whatever grievances you may have against one another. Forgive as the Lord forgave you. And over all these virtues put on love, which binds them all together in perfect unity' (Col. 3:12-14, NIV).

Adoption is discovered in its full bloom in our experience as we share its outworking in the local church family and as we look forward to its consummation in the next world. That world will be a world of love and of knowing God. In view of these facts we should strive for Christian love to abound in the churches to which we belong, as well as in any other Christian associations that we may sustain. This family love contributes enormously to the life, vigour, effectiveness and growth of a church. We can well understand the assertion of John Owen when he says, 'A church full of love, is a church well built up. I had rather see a church filled with love a thousand times, than filled with the best, the highest, and most glorious gifts and parts that any men in this world may be partakers of.'

Money, organisation, activity, talent, testimonies, sermons and special efforts are all rendered futile when the testimony of a church is destroyed by strife within. But when genuine love prevails the potential and possibilities are unbounded. Our Lord said, 'By *this* shall all men know that you are my disciples, if ye have love one to another' (John 13:35).

In conclusion may I ask you some personal questions? Have you been adopted into this family of love? If so what has your contribution been toward family unity? How rich is your own experience of adoption in your daily walk as a family member? How warm is your appreciation of the experience of other brothers and sisters in the family? And finally, are you going to contribute more to the Christian family because you have read this exposition?

Chapter 13

Assurance in our Experience

THE subject of assurance of salvation belongs very much to the category of experience. Negatively, this can be seen when a believer is in doubt about his salvation. Such doubt can easily give way to depression, and even unhappiness or grief. What misery there is in not being sure that one will escape the fires of eternal torment! Positively, a well-grounded and strong assurance can be attended with joy unspeakable, a peace which passes understanding and many sweet, spiritual comforts. This is especially the case when the believer is able to contemplate with confidence his 'inheritance incorruptible and undefiled, and that fadeth not away, reserved' in heaven for him (1 Pet. 1:4). What intense joy belongs to those who have a well-grounded assurance of salvation. As we have seen, the clearer their views of justification the better the joy. If the great God declares our righteousness we can rejoice forever more.

William Guthrie regarded assurance as 'the Christian's great interest' and gave that title to his classic on the subject. This is an apt description, for the attainment of certainty of our place in heaven is certainly our greatest personal interest in this world.

The Scriptures not only speak clearly on this subject but also urge the enjoyment of a well-grounded assurance. 'These things have I written unto you that believe on the name of the Son of God; that ye may know that ye have eternal life.' And such is our assurance that we know that he hears our prayers and that he will answer them (1 John 5:13,14; John 15:7). On the other hand, a wavering man will receive nothing (Jas. 1:6,7). The attaining of assurance enriches Christian experience and will, according to Thomas Brooks, produce heaven upon earth, sweeten life's changes, assist communion with God, preserve from backsliding, produce holy boldness, prepare for death and lead to enjoyment of Christ.

This matter of assurance is one which has been more hotly contested than most Christians realize. Even the Reformers and Puritans, who are rightly regarded as theological giants in the history of the Church, differed among themselves on this subject.

John Calvin, as we would expect, with characteristic clarity of expression expounded the doctrine of assurance. In so doing he was representative of the Reformers who repudiated in no uncertain terms the Roman Catholic idea that faith can be regarded as mere assent or notion. The Holy Spirit, author of the new birth, is the author of faith, a living faith which unites the believer to Christ. To the Reformers, belief in Christ was to be joined to Christ. Faith was to see Christ with believing eyes. So to believe was in fact to be assured of Christ. Thus faith and assurance were brought into the closest possible proximity. To be assured, the believer looked to Christ as the only source of all his blessing and the only source of eternal life. Assurance was not to be found by the believer looking within himself or looking to his own piety. Calvin deplored a man looking at his own holiness to conclude he had faith. He did not recognise any kind of faith that did not of itself assure. He saw a total reciprocity between the Spirit, who imparts faith, and Christ, the object of faith. For Calvin, faith was a direct knowledge of God. 'Christ, then, is the mirror in which we ought, and which, without deception, we may contemplate our election' (*Inst.* 3. 24:5).

The Puritans, in contrast to the Reformers, while not denying the primacy of the direct witness of the Spirit, taught that assurance is also to be based on the believer's sanctification (by looking to the holiness of the believer). The quintessence of their teaching as a body of divines is expressed in the Westminster Confession of Faith (1643) and the 1689 Baptist Confession (cf. ch. 18). Goodwin, Rutherford, William Bridge, Thomas Brooks and Thomas Watson were among those who handled the theme with insight and penetration. When it came to self-examination they were fully aware of the dangers of legalism and introspection.

Mainly because of modern evangelistic methods which result in much false assurance and ultimate disillusionment, we have need of discernment about assurance. The care and thoroughness exemplified by the Puritan expositions provide a rich source of material and guidance for us. Why did they deem the subject to be so important? How did they answer the allegation that assurance based on sanctification tends to legalism? Were they correct in believing that for wise reasons God withdraws assurance? Should we or should we not challenge that idea with vigour? What counsel, and in particular, what remedies did they prescribe for those lacking assurance?

The only way in which we can do justice to such questions is to follow the example of these our forefathers and know the Scriptures well enough to be able to decide such matters for ourselves. I propose, therefore, to define assurance and then provide a survey of what the Scriptures teach about the subject.

After that we can look at the effects of assurance in experience and answer some pointed questions about the matter.

1. *Assurance defined*

As the word suggests, assurance has simply to do with being sure. We believe in Christ and we are sure that he will save us. Scripture describes faith as 'assurance of things hoped for, a conviction of things not seen' (Heb. 11:1, A.R.V.). Abraham was fully persuaded (assured) that what God had promised, he was able also to perform. Assurance means confidence. It also means a full conviction, translated *full assurance* in the King James Version (1 Thess. 1:5; Col. 2:2; Heb. 6:11; 10:22). Assurance is a conviction for which reasons can be given. It concerns facts. Feelings and emotions about these facts enter in, but assurance is more than feelings. We can feel depressed and discouraged about our spiritual condition and yet know at the same time with certainty that we have eternal life. Assurance does not bypass the understanding. Paul speaks of a 'full assurance of understanding' (Col. 2:2).

The word assurance has always been used in the sense of our being sure about our personal salvation for the simple reason that no other word expresses more simply what is at stake. Those denominations which are described as sacramental are not sympathetic to the idea of assurance of salvation. Their system of belief and practice points to reliance upon the Church, priests, the saints, the sacraments and upon good works performed, rather than on Christ who alone can save with absolute certainty and finality. The person who trusts in such foundations for his salvation may have a slender hope, but the system discourages an absolute certainty or the declaration of an infallible assurance.

Arminians are unable to develop consistent teaching about assurance because they reject the doctrine of the perseverance of the saints. If it is accepted that a person can become a true believer, that is regenerate, and then so fall away as to be unregenerate and lost, it follows that there can never be a well-grounded assurance of salvation. Those in the Reformation tradition hold to the primacy of regeneration. God alone is the author of the new birth. By his word he quickens whom he wills. Once regenerate, the believer can never be unregenerate. The good work begun by God will be completed by him (Phil. 1:6). However, allowance must be made for those called temporary believers, people who are subject to a work of the Spirit which falls short of the new birth. In defining assurance, it will help to examine the relationship of assurance to hope, to faith and to sanctification.

Firstly, what is the relationship between hope and assurance? Hope may be defined as a gift of God whereby we are given the expectation of good to come. Hope is objective in that it is centred in God himself. The ground of the hope of eternal life is the same for the experienced Christian as for the beginner. We lay hold of the hope set before us, that is we lay hold upon Christ who is our hope (Heb. 6:18). When he who is our hope returns, our redemption will be complete. Hope will then be no more since it will have been realised (Rom. 8:24,25). The apostles themselves, during Christ's ministry on earth, were confused about the future state. The resurrection of Christ changed that and their hope became very clear, not of an earthly kingdom but of eternal glory. Believers are born again to a living hope which means that the contemplation of the hope imparts strength and life. It inspires discipline. 'Every man that hath this hope in him purifieth himself' (1 John 3:3). It inspires endurance in suffering too. 'Others were tortured, not accepting deliverance; that they might obtain a better resurrection' (Heb. 11:35). While hope is objective, having its object in heaven, assurance is subjective inasmuch as assurance is the inward persuasion or conviction that that hope of glory is really possessed and that nothing can take it away.

Secondly, what is the relationship between faith and assurance? Saving faith is an action of belief and trust exercised by the understanding and will whereby the believer is joined to Christ in a state of reliance upon him. Assurance is a reflexive act in which the believer stands back and sees himself to be in a state of happy union with Christ. Faith comes first and brings assurance in its wake. Faith can be likened to seeing Christ. By faith we see him and believe in him, and then, seeing and believing, we cannot but be assured of our union with him. If we believe in this way, how can

we not have assurance?   The answer is that in reality and experience
faith is not always as clear or as vigorous as that.   Dark clouds can
hide the vision of the unseen world where Christ ever lives to intercede for us.

Thirdly, what relationship does assurance have to sanctification,
which is that work of the Holy Spirit within us to make us holy and
conform us to Christ?   Since the same Holy Spirit who sanctifies us
also assures us, is it right to base assurance upon the observation that
God is working in us both to will and do his good pleasure?   The
answer is yes, since both justification and sanctification are the gifts
of God.   A right discernment of God's gifts and of the Spirit's work
within us strengthens assurance.   Spiritual discernment is needed
to make sure that our practice of truth, our loving the brethren and
our doing works of righteousness are really inspired and motivated
by the Holy Spirit and are not the product of self-interest or self-
righteousness.   The discernment of such issues has much to do with
a well-grounded assurance of salvation.

2. *What the Scriptures teach about assurance*

Old Testament believers expressed their assurance of salvation in a
forthright way.   'I know that my redeemer liveth,' said Job asserting
his redemption, and 'in my flesh shall I see God' (Job 19:25,26).
A strong personal assurance was encouraged by the words of God to
the patriarch, 'Fear not, Abram: I am thy shield, and thy exceeding
great reward.'   What an astonishing statement!   What doubt could
remain about eternal life if God was Abraham's exceeding great
reward.   Consider expressions in the Psalms, 'For this God is our
God for ever and ever' (Ps. 48:14) and 'Thou shalt guide me with
thy counsel, and afterward receive me to glory' (Ps. 73:24).

Statements about assurance are found in profusion throughout
the New Testament.   A verse which both defines and summarises
the matter is 2 Timothy 1:12; 'I know whom I have believed, and
am persuaded that he is able to keep that which I have committed
unto him against that day.'   In addition there are many passages
which encourage assurance, such as our Lord's promise 'And I give

unto them eternal life; and they shall never perish, neither shall any man pluck them out of my hand' (John 10:28).

If we stand back and view this subject in perspective I believe that in order of priority we should proceed from the Johanine statements to Romans 8, to Hebrews and finally to John's epistle as follows: (i) Our Lord's promise of the Holy Spirit (John 14: 16,17) and Paul's exposition of life in the Spirit in Romans chapter eight. (ii) The problem of false assurance as portrayed in the epistle to the Hebrews. (iii) Factors to support a well-grounded assurance as expressed by John in his first epistle. These Scriptures I regard as providing the main New Testament data from which we may establish the doctrine.

(i)   Our Lord's promise of the Holy Spirit (Jn. 14:16,17) and Romans chapter eight

Our Lord's brief, physical presence on earth was unique. The privilege of seeing him and the comfort of being able to converse with him and receive counsel from him can hardly be over-estimated. Little wonder that the apostles clung to his physical presence and refused to receive or accept the clearest statements repeatedly made by him about his impending death and ascension to his Father. He told them plainly just before the event that he would be crucified but they did not want to believe it (Matt. 26:2).

In preparing them for the trauma of his humiliating death and to equip them for their ministries which would follow, he told them that the coming of the Holy Spirit would be better than his physical presence with them. He and the Father would send the Holy Spirit to dwell in them for ever (Jn. 14:16,17). The implications for assurance of the indwelling of the Holy Spirit are enormous. Having implanted faith in the heart, the Spirit guides, teaches, comforts, prompts and assures the believer. In place of clinging to Christ's physical presence they were encouraged to depend on the Holy Spirit. The word rendered 'comforter' (paraclete) literally means 'one called to be beside another'. As an advocate stands beside his client to assure him, so the Holy Spirit supports the believer making his cause his own. If a person says that he knows he has eternal life because God's Spirit within tells him so, you have only his word for it. That person is giving witness to something within which others cannot test. But the Spirit does not only assure in that particular way. At the same time he teaches and inspires a holy life. He does not do the one without the other. The person testifying to an inward witness of the Holy Spirit should at the same time evidence the work of the Spirit in his general behaviour.   Our Lord told his disciples that the Spirit would not only dwell in them as an advocate to assure but he would teach, instruct and assist them. The Holy Spirit did this work so well that the world was turned upside down by them.   Whatever personal testimony was borne by the apostles to eternal life, it was supported by outward evidence of the reality of the Spirit dwelling within.

With that in mind we turn to Romans chapter eight.   This chapter has been called the charter of Christian assurance.   It begins with the assurance for those in Christ of *no condemnation* and ends with the assurance of *no separation* from Christ.   But how can we know that we are 'in Christ'?   The theme of the chapter is life in the Spirit.   We know that we are in Christ because we live a spiritual life (8:1), have been made free from the bondage of sin (8:2), are spiritually minded (8:6), mortify the deeds of the body (8:13), are led by the Spirit (8:14), have received the Spirit of adoption (8:15), have the witness in our hearts that we are God's children (8:16), and are enabled to pray (8:26,27).   All this, and the consideration of God's sovereign unchangeable purpose in Christ, results in a strong persuasion or assurance that nothing in the universe can separate us from Christ (8:38,39).

The peak to which Paul ascends in his reasoning is one of the highest in Scripture.   If God has loved us from eternity, predestinated us, called us and justified us – who will annul the blessing?   If God justifies us, not all the devils in the universe can change that and nothing whatever can separate us from the love of God.

If we examine the varying aspects referred to above we will see that there is that in which we are passive, 'the Spirit himself beareth witness with our spirit that we are the children of God'.   There is also that in which we are active.   The Holy Spirit works in believers to make them active in prayer, active in mortifying sin, and applying discipline to their daily walk and active in choosing paths of righteousness.   Whatever the activities, there is always the passive element in which the believer bears in his heart at all times the inward testimony of adoption, that he is an heir of eternal life.   But this inward testimony should never in any way contradict, restrict or circumscribe the prompting of the Spirit to an activity of holy living.   Indeed, the stronger inward assurance of adoption the more likely are the other aspects of experience to flourish, including mortification of the flesh.   We can suspect a testimony of inward assurance to eternal life to be false if there is not a commensurate testimony of holy living.   The possibility of self-deception and false assurance is very real.

(ii) The problem of false assurance as portrayed in the epistle to the Hebrews

Our faith, and hence our assurance, is bound to be tested and tried. The epistle to the Hebrews reveals that there were those who, having made a full profession of faith, having been 'enlightened', having 'tasted of the heavenly gift', and having been 'made partakers of the Holy Ghost', were in danger of falling away (Heb. 6:4-6). C. H. Spurgeon in preaching on this took the 'if' of verse six in our Authorised Version and delivered the whole of his sermon on the basis of hypothesis.   The 'if' is not in the original!   Apostasy is a reality, it happened then and it happens today.   There have always been some who, after having been set apart (sanctified) by the blood of the covenant (having been integrated into the life of the church), have trodden underfoot all that they professed before to be sacred and essential to their salvation (Heb. 10:29).   The road to apostasy is a road taken gradually.   It shows by a decline in assembling with other believers.   Apostasy from faith in Christ is the burden of Hebrews, forsaking the assembling together of the saints being one of the main symptoms (Heb. 10:25).   We are reminded of the reality of apostasy by such names as Saul, Judas, Balaam and Demas.

If, in what can be described as the two climactic passages of Hebrews (Heb. 6:4-11 and 10:22-39), we read of those who fall away, does not this underline our responsibility 'to make our calling and election sure?'   In view of this fearful danger what is the safeguard prescribed by the author of Hebrews?   In the first passage he commands diligence in attaining a 'full assurance of hope' (Heb. 6:11).   In the second there is the exhortation to draw near in 'full assurance of faith' (Heb. 10:22).

Full assurance of faith (Heb. 10:22) consists of firm, robust and unwavering persuasion that Jesus Christ is the King of glory, the prophet divine and the great high priest who ever mediates for us. The epistle sets forth Christ in a way designed to establish an immovable faith in him.   This theme of faith, applied at the end of the tenth chapter, is illustrated in the famous eleventh chapter and finally driven home at the beginning of the twelfth chapter.   The subject of assurance is asserted in verse thirty-five, 'cast not away your confidence' (*parrhesia*).   This confidence is a boldness – a strong prevailing persuasion or assurance of our acceptance with God.

The full assurance of hope (Heb. 6:11) to be diligently sought is a

strong confidence that the hope set before us will be realised.   The
'full assurance' (*plerophoria*) means an assurance which has been
filled up with strength – a dynamic assurance!   A little hope will
preserve a man from total apostasy but a 'full assurance', an un-
shakable confidence, an immovable conviction, will carry a man
through flood and fire, through trial and tribulation.

It is significant that the attainment of such a powerful assurance,
according to the Hebrew epistle, is not to be sought by a quest for
indefinable mystical experiences but by diligence in the discipline
attending our warfare (Heb. 6:11,12).   As a soldier fights on the
battlefield by relentless attention to fitness, discipline, watchfulness
and care about his armour and weapons so must we be as watchful
and disciplined in our spiritual warfare.   The outcome depends on
this.

The bond or union between faith, practice and assurance in
Hebrews is apparent.   The primary objective of the writer is to
combat the temptation to forsake faith in Christ and faithful Christian practice and to return to trust in and practice of the Old
Testament system.   But Christ is the fulfilment of the Old Testament
system and greater than Moses and Aaron.   The stronger and
clearer our faith in Christ, the more zealous will be our adherence
to his teaching, obedience to his precepts and identification with his
people.   The stronger and clearer our faith and faithfulness in
practice the stronger and clearer our assurance.   How is faith in
Christ strengthened?   By diligent attention to the means of grace.
Faith, practice and assurance are triplets, the best friends, always
helping and strengthening one another.   No place is found in
Scripture and no quarter given to any kind of assurance which is
divorced from faith and practice.

(*iii*) *Factors to support a well-grounded assurance as expressed by John in
    his first epistle*

The understanding of what is otherwise a very difficult epistle is
wonderfully facilitated when we grasp that John's aim throughout is
to expose and refute Gnosticism, which in the event became one of
the greatest forces ever to oppose the Gospel.   The *Gnosis* or knowledge, by which the movement became known, points to its specific
character.   The Gnostics claimed an esoteric knowledge, that is a
special knowledge possessed only by the initiated or an elete group.
'We know' was their boast, but they were destitute of spiritual
dynamic and no equivalent moral virtue existed to support their

specious and deceitful claim. Gnosticism was a form of intellectualism without holiness. As a philosophy it was similar to evolution, only in reverse. Present-day evolution starts with slime, and stage by stage from there goes up to higher forms and eventually reaches the apex in man. Gnosticism started with God as the highest point, then descended to the angels and the spirit world and finally arrived at the lowest form which was the flesh of man. To the Gnostics the flesh was essentially sinful. Jesus could not have been a man, they reasoned, because flesh is evil. They separated man into two storeys. The upper storey consisted of the spirit and the lower storey of the flesh. The flesh could break every law and indulge every lust because it was a separate entity from the spirit which could soar aloft. The spirit, they claimed, was without sin. Thus they were antinomian (anti-law, anti-moral) in practice.

With this devilish teaching threatening to undermine the churches (1 John 2:26) we can appreciate the decisiveness of John's approach when he repeatedly asserts 'we know'. They, the Gnostics, say, 'they know'. They claim a special knowledge, but 'we know', and our knowledge is a knowledge that stands up to searching tests. If any man claims to be sure of salvation he must at the same time be ready for tests. Let him prove his faith and verify his assurance with a consistent Christian walk (1 John 2:4-6).

John does not deny the direct witness of the Holy Spirit in the heart of the believer. Indeed an assurance of union with Christ and with the Father expressly by the Spirit dwelling within is foremost in John's teaching, as it is in Paul's. 'Hereby know we that we dwell in him, and he in us, because he hath given us of his Spirit' (1 John 4:13). To be in Christ and to possess the Spirit, in contrast to having a mere intellectual knowledge, is fundamental for the believer. Christianity is all about the life of God in the soul of man. We are partakers of the divine nature (2 Pet. 1:4). John links a knowledge of the Holy Spirit within us with the life which the Spirit manifests, namely, love for the brethren (1 John 4:12), and keeping God's commandments (1 John 3:24).

Such is the person, work and power of the Spirit dwelling in believers that they cannot but recognise him and know by his presence and work that they are in Christ. As Paul asserts, the Holy Spirit indwelling us is the earnest or guarantee of our adoption, our inheritance and eternal life (2 Cor. 1:22 and 5:5; Eph. 1:14). The Spirit himself witnesses with our spirit that we are children of God. John encourages believers to recognise the Holy Spirit who indwells them, but we ought to note very well that at the same time he refers to the effects of the indwelling of the same Holy Spirit, namely, respect for the commandments (1 John 3:24) and love for God's family (1 John 4:12). So important does he deem this principle (a holy life the evidence of the Spirit's work within) that he does not hesitate to repeat it in different ways.

The Gnostics said 'we know' and stopped at that. They were hostile to holiness, opposed to the commandments, were loveless, unbrotherly, carnal and denied the truth of the incarnation of Christ. John set to work and showed that in contrast to their 'we know', the Christian 'we know' is practical. The indwelling of the Holy Spirit must, without fail, be evidenced by love for what God loves. We should love his holy and inscrutable law. We should love his Son who kept and fulfilled that law for us and died for those who have transgressed it. We should love the Lord's people. If we do not, we have no right to assurance of salvation. A pretence to assurance of eternal life, therefore, which is unaccompanied by spiritual life flowing from the indwelling power of the Spirit within, is spurious – it is mere head-knowledge – a form of gnosticism, empty, vain and delusive.

We must now face the question of whether it is valid to base our assurance on sanctification. In refuting the Gnostic heresy John insists that believers not only have the Spirit but they possess the life of the Spirit. This life of holiness can and must be tested. He applies three tests, the social, the doctrinal and the moral. The Gnostics say they know but 'we know that we have passed from death unto life, because we love the brethren' (1 John 3:14). It is perfectly in order to deduce that we are part of God's family by the observation that we have been given a new nature, a nature which goes out toward and loves the communion of saints, the fellowship of heaven. We can remember the time when we detested and abhorred such company.

Loving the brethren, or the social test, features strongly in the epistle. There are also the doctrinal and moral tests, believing rightly and practising correctly. Faith to believe in Christ as 'God manifest in the flesh' is God's gift, a gift to be recognised and cherished (Eph. 2:8,9; Heb. 12:2; 2 Pet. 1:1). Likewise good works are the gift of God (Eph. 2:10).

The first principle of the Gospel is that we are justified by faith not by works. The second principle is that true faith results in good works (Jas. 2:24). Hence, Peter declares that if we are diligent to add works to our faith we shall never fall (2 Pet. 1:5-10).

A well-grounded assurance of eternal life, then, is based upon the free grace of God, his gift of the Holy Spirit, his gift of faith and his gift of good works which accompany salvation. We ought not to stress any one feature at the expense of another. We cannot afford to be negligent in any way. We cannot afford to forsake the assembling of ourselves together. We neglect the good works of faith at our peril. Does not dependence upon good works in this way encourage legalism? Undoubtedly there is always the danger of legalism, stronger in some than in others, but there is a world of difference between a disposition that serves God out of love and thankfulness for salvation (John 14:23), and a disposition of self-righteousness in the person who seeks to do good in order to earn salvation or prove that he is saved.

In my view, a well-grounded assurance is based firstly on the inward witness of the Holy Spirit testifying to sonship. Secondly, and no less essentially, it is based on a spiritual life which is in harmony with sonship, not one or the other, but both together. If there is a deficiency in the heart or deficiency in the life then the believer should seek both the Lord himself and the means of grace to make good that deficiency. A whole area of counsel from Scripture opens up when we begin to deal with reasons for lack of assurance and remedies drawn from Scripture to meet the lack. Using the Scriptures that have been cited we ought to be in a position to help those who have problems with assurance, but now we will go on and examine the effects of assurance upon Christian experience.

How assurance affects experience

W̶HAT is man's chief end? Man's chief end is to know God and enjoy him forever. Justified and cleansed, with a true heart we approach God with a full assurance of faith. Such full assurance enables us to pray with boldness (Heb. 4:16; 10:19). When a believer can say, 'The life I now live, I live by faith in the Son of God who loved me and gave himself for me', he has a sure foundation for communion. The love of Christ shown in his dying in our place must always be the source of our love to him. That is our first love from which we must never depart (Rev. 2:4). The assurance of Christ's love sweetens communion, as illustrated in the Song of Solomon, 'I sat down under his shadow with great delight, and his fruit was sweet to my taste. He brought me to the banqueting house, and his banner over me was love' (S. of S. 2:3,4). The assurance of spiritual union is 'my beloved is mine, and I am his' (S. of S. 2:16). Assurance enriches the enjoyment of our religion and enjoyment helps make us strong in the exercise and practice of our religion. The athlete who sets about his training with zeal and zest because he loves it is likely to progress more than one who does not. Likewise, a craftsman who adores and enjoys his craft is likely to excel. Let us take these illustrations a step further. Suppose that both the athlete and craftsman are gifted and know it, will that confidence help or hinder them? Providing it is assurance and not arrogance it will help them. Turning from the natural to the spiritual, if we are assured we have the gift of saving faith we will exercise that gift the more, will enjoy communion more, and enjoy our religion more, and thus be stronger in the practice of it.

As with the Son so with the Father, the assurance of his love helps communion. The Authorised Version omits an important statement in 1 John 3:1. 'Behold, what manner of love the Father hath bestowed upon us, that we should be called the sons of God.' Some manuscripts include 'and so we are!' There is no doubt about it! We are the children of our Father and we love him and worship him in gratitude for he has loved us while we were yet sinners, sent his Son to die for us, and has blessed us with all spiritual blessings in Christ. These blessings of the Father include election, predestination, calling, justification and ultimately the completion of our redemption in the glorification of the body.

To lack assurance is to cast a doubt upon all these blessings as they apply to us personally. How can we enjoy the author of the blessings if we constantly doubt our personal interest in them? On the other hand the stronger the assurance of our union with the Trinity the better and richer will be our communion with the Trinity. Also, our fellowship with the fellow-heirs of so great salvation will be warmer by reason of the assurance we enjoy together. Our assurance is a confirmation to them of the reality of the Gospel.

The more assurance of the hope of eternal life among believers, the warmer, stronger and sweeter will be the sharing of that hope. Our conversation (citizenship) is in heaven. The better our assurance of that citizenship the more spiritual fellowship will be encouraged with increased love and tenderness and, to use the words of Thomas Brooks, 'the less noise, less contention, less distraction, less biting, and less devouring among the saints'.

When we experience tribulation, assurance will enable us to view our present afflictions as light compared to the far more exceeding and eternal weight of glory which is ours (2 Cor. 4:17). Observe the assurance of Paul's language in the face of affliction, '*We know*', he says, 'that we have a house eternal in the heavens.' When physical weaknesses increase and when we are obliged, with sorrow, to lay aside the privileges of work and service which have given us much pleasure and fulfilment, even then the assurance of a better world, and of an inheritance incorruptible reserved in heaven for us, will comfort us and as Brooks aptly says, 'sweeten life's changes'.

If we are to be overrun, as other countries have been, and fall into the hands of persecutors, what then? Will not the assurance of eternal life and assurance of the promise that he will never leave us nor forsake us add to our strength and comfort?

We need to use the whole armour of God and have the assurance of victory when temptations assail us and we find ourselves wrestling with principalities and powers. The symbol of this is the helmet of salvation. In battle the helmet not only provided protection but it bore the regimental colours and army rank. If Caesar's troops attacked a city there was no doubt about the Emperor they represented and neither was there any doubt concerning discipline, loyalty and valour. Were they not the conquerors of the world? But the captain of our salvation has made conquest not only of the world but over sin, death, hell and the grave. Whatever cuts, bruises, scars and wounds we receive in battle, the helmet reminds us that Christ is our hope and he cannot fail. The helmet also assures us that, no matter how bloody the skirmishes, the war will be won. The captain of our salvation has secured victory. We are to be diligent therefore to attain 'the full assurance of hope unto the end' (Heb. 6:11). A full assurance of hope will strengthen the saint in death. As dying Stephen saw the Lord standing at the right hand of God, so a full assurance will enable the Christian to despise the pains of death, defy the fear of death and resist the accusations of Satan. He will see Christ in the Word as his justification and redemption. Confident and fully assured that the good work begun in him by God omnipotent will be completed infallibly, the assured believer will fight a good fight, keep the faith, finish his course and know that a crown of life incorruptible shall be given him in that great coming day (1 Cor. 9:25; 2 Tim. 4:7,8).

As we have seen, assurance of salvation in this life is of inestimable value. Thomas Watson extols its worth in glowing terms:

How sweet it is. This is the manna in the golden pot; the white stone, the wine of paradise which cheers the heart. How comfortable is God's smile! The sun is more refreshing when it shines out than when it is hid in a cloud; it is a prelibation and a foretaste of glory, it puts a man in heaven before his time. None can know how delicious and ravishing it is, but such as have felt it; as none can know how sweet honey is, but they who have tasted it.[1]

The possibility of having a false assurance is the foremost reason why this subject demands thoughtful care. Many deceive themselves and many also think they have done wonderful things in Christ's name will be exposed as self-deceived in the great day of judgment (Matt. 7:22,23).

Let us be thorough then in our study as we turn attention to answering some of the questions that can be asked with regard to assurance.

Some pointed questions answered

If we base our assurance on our sanctification does this not lead to legalism?

In reply to this question we should remember that justification and sanctification are joined inseparably. Paul repudiates with some indignation the idea that we can be justified by faith and yet not have sanctification. Union with Christ by faith achieves both the imputation of Christ's righteousness to the believer as well as the life of the Spirit (Rom. 6:4-6). It therefore follows that our profession of Christianity must stand up to examination in all respects – faith (what is believed), experience and practice. Said James, faith without works is dead, being alone. This does not mean that we concentrate on good works alone and rely on that as a foundation of assurance. Rather we recognise that both faith and good works are the gifts of God. As we live out a life of obedience we recognise that opportunities afforded for good works are given by God (Eph. 2:10) and being ordained to these we are to seize the opportunities with gladness.

William Bridge calls for what he terms the visible characters of justification so that when a believer sees them he may say, 'Surely here is sanctification, that is no other than that which flows from free remission, and justification by faith alone!'[2]

There is a world of difference between doing good works on a legalistic basis of trying to make ourselves worthy to be good enough for God to accept, and good works out of love because we are God's children. Rendering service in an evangelical spirit of gratitude to God our Father for so great salvation is basic to our Christianity. The recognition day by day of the good works that are given us to do (Eph. 2:10) is a confirmation of our union with Christ which we cannot help but recognise.

An all-round healthy condition spiritually is an excellent strength to assurance and can be likened to physical fitness. An athlete is confident when his physique passes all the tests. If the heart or the digestion or the limbs falter his performance is immediately in jeopardy. He cannot assure himself by saying, 'well everything is in good shape except for my heart – I will be okay!' No! He must pass an all round fitness test if he is to be sure. Likewise it is no good for a professing believer to say that he feels really good inside and enjoys a direct assurance by the Holy Spirit from heaven if at the same time we find him full of malice toward other believers, or swearing at his wife and children, or neglecting his local church, or stealing from his firm. It is essential to view the Christian life in the wholeness of its expression and not be content with satisfaction or growth in some areas only. The point is illustrated by Peter's exhortation when he says, 'Make every effort to supplement your faith with virtue, and virtue with knowledge, and knowledge with steadfastness, and steadfastness with godliness, and godliness with brotherly affection, and brotherly affection with love' (2 Pet. 1:5-7 R.S.V.).

Thomas Brooks in similar vein is very comprehensive in expounding on ways and means to gain a well-grounded assurance. As the things which accompany salvation he lays special stress upon, faith, repentance, obedience, love, prayer, perseverance and hope.

Providing then that salvation is viewed in its wholeness as flowing from the fountainhead of free grace, legalism will be averted. Repentance is an ongoing activity in the experience of the christian and is to be viewed both in its inception and progress as the gift of God. Good works stem from God's free grace. All is of grace. Christ is made to us wisdom and righteousness and sanctification and redemption. If we seek to be motivated by the glory of God in all our actions and attribute all that is good in ourselves and others to his free grace, we shall be preserved from legalism.

Does God withhold assurance from some believers?

Thomas Brooks suggests seven reasons why God denies assurance for a time to some believers. These can be paraphrased as follows: 1. For the exercise of grace,   2. To keep believers in the exercise of their religious duties,   3. That they may be more clearly convinced of the evil of sin,   4. That they may learn to seek assurance for his honour and glory and not for selfish reasons,   5. That when they have assurance they may more highly prize it,   6. That they may be kept humble,   7. That they may live by faith in Christ.

I find myself disagreeing with Brooks throughout this section and question the legitimacy of speaking in these terms.   I maintain that it is God's revealed will that all his children should enjoy assurance. Therefore the propriety of talking about wise reasons for God's withholding of assurance is to be challenged.   Brooks offers little proof from Scripture, and where he does the passages are either irrelevant or else they refer to desertion and not to assurance.[3]

The distinction between desertion and assurance must be kept very clear in our minds.   Assurance is that knowledge within us that we are God's children.   Desertion is when we lack any felt presence or comfort from God.   Job felt utterly deserted by God and complained most bitterly about it, but he never doubted for one minute that he belonged to God.   Likewise Christ was totally deserted of the felt approbation and presence of God and cried in anguish, 'Why hast thou forsaken me?' – but he did say '*my* God!' Never was there the slightest doubt about his Sonship.

Now God may withdraw his comforting or felt presence for the reasons proposed by Brooks but where in the Scripture does it speak at all about God withholding assurance?   There are many reasons why some do not attain assurance but it is certainly very unhealthy to build up a system of thinking in which we attribute lack of assurance to God.   Some lack assurance because they feel condemned by their own sins and their faith cannot rise to the free justification held out in the Gospel.   Some may lack assurance because of lack of clarity about the doctrine of justification.   Others may lack because they do rely upon their own performance not placing their works within the context of justification.   Others may lack assurance because of their neglect of the means of grace and because of carelessness.

The promises of God concerning the gift of the Holy Spirit and with him the assurance of sonship are yea and Amen. To promote a philosophy of reasons why this should not really be so is to fall short of the mark. Much as we value the Puritans and esteem their expositions we will not follow them where we find Scriptural support to be lacking.

A parallel to this can be seen in the subject of the Gospel invitations. I was truly amazed recently to hear a young man say that God commands all men everywhere to repent but that he does not really want them to repent. He said, 'we must not give them the impression that God wants them to repent! We must command but not beseech sinners to repent. Now our case would indeed be sad if we were for one moment to submit to such outrageous reasoning. Of course God desires that all men should repent. If we felt that it was not so then we would immediately follow suit and not desire their repentance ourselves. Our invitation would be paralysed at its very source. Of course men will not repent of themselves but their unwillingness does not change in the least God's desire, and ours, that they do what is right and turn. Nor does the fact that God has determined sovereignly to bring about the repentance of many, change his desire for all.

In the matter of assurance there never is any doubt but that a full assurance of sonship is God's desire for all his children. If he needs to chastise them he does it on other ways than the withdrawal of assurance because assurance is a matter of great moment. The withdrawal of it is akin to the withdrawal of salvation. Does he not say, 'and I give unto them eternal life and they shall never perish, neither shall any man pluck them out of my hand'?

Thomas Goodwin puts the matter well when he says, 'there be times of desertion, when God, to make us look better to our footing, leaves us a little, as if he would forsake us, when indeed he leaves us to draw us after him, to cleave more closely to him; for this shaking is to settle us deeper![4] The two passages in the Song of Solomon, 3:1-6 and 5:1-9, perfectly illustrate the point. It would be preposterous for the bridegroom to say, 'I wish to withdraw from you the knowledge in your heart that we belong to each other for time

---

Footnotes to 'Some pointed questions answered'

[1] *Body of Divinity*, Thomas Watson, p. 253.
[2] William Bridge, *Works*, vol. 1, p. 336 ff.
[3] *Heaven on Earth* (paperback edition) p. 33. Some of the Scriptures put forward are Lam. 1:16, 3:2,3; 2 Cor. 12:7-9; Heb. 11:7; Matt. 25:4-6; Jer. 2:19; Ps. 4:7; John 2:2; Ps. 139:8; all of which have to do with experience but not the removal of sonship.
[4] Thomas Goodwin, *Works*, vol. 3, p. 467.

and eternity.'

Much rather does he withdraw his presence for wise reasons – his presence – yes, assurance, never!

The Teaching of the Reformers and Puritans

One's thinking on a subject like assurance develops over years and is influenced primarily by the exercise of having to preach in a systematic, expository fashion three times a week.   Conferences such as the annual Puritan Conference (now called the Westminster Conference) in London; discussion with other ministers; and especially practical pastoral experience all contribute.   But correspondence also has an important rôle. I would like to acknowledge the help afforded me by Bob Letham with regard to sources of reference as far as the Reformers are concerned and to provide an example of the help afforded by correspondence.   I am including a letter from Peter Lewis just as it was received without any refinements.

Dear Erroll,

In your series of articles on experience (*Ref. Today* 30) you wrote on the subject of Assurance concluding with a description of the teaching of the Reformers and Puritans.   I thought that you could have enlarged that more than you did and have discussed this with you by phone.   You said that you would welcome further references on the theme.

I would like to stress differences in emphases existed among the Reformers and Puritans throughout their times.   This has always been well known.   For instance, Le Blanc wrote of these differences in detail in the seventeenth century and Cunningham did so in the nineteenth; and much close work has been done in our own.   This difference appeared almost from the beginning.   Some of the Reformers (eg. Luther and Calvin) in strong reaction to Rome, defined true and saving faith as always and essentially possessing a notable degree of certitude and assurance.   Others among the Reformers (eg. Martyr, Musculus, Zanchius) in response to the pastoral facts of life sought to correct any extreme position and distinguished between faith, and assurance as its consequence (rather than as of its essence).   In the development of the debate, this latter viewpoint became dominant in English Reformed and Puritan theology.

Nevertheless, the difference was always one of emphasis rather than of principle.   On the one hand, while Calvin maintained that saving faith had within itself confidence and certitude (*Inst.* book 3, chap. 2, sectns. 15, 16), he also recognised that Christians did often lack assurance and might begin with various and varying degrees of it (sectns. 17-20).   On the other hand, those who differed from him in emphasis and expression –

and this includes the English Puritans generally – were yet quite prepared to accept that faith had within itself an essential, germinal assurance that might simply pass unrecognised by the holder of it in his reflections upon his state; for, as they all held, at regeneration the Spirit communicates *himself* with all his powers and graces, and therefore the new-born Christian has within himself the root or seed or germ of all the graces – including, of course, assurance! Thus a bridge always existed uniting the two views. *A man may have assurance and not know that he has it.* William Ames was quite aware of this bridge and of the essential unity of the parties: 'This justifying faith, *of its own nature* doth produce, and so hath joined with it a special and certain persuasion of the grace and mercy of God in Christ: whence also justifying faith is oftentimes not amiss described by the orthodox [Calvin!] by this persuasion, especially when they do oppose that general faith to which the Papists ascribe all things: but (1) This persuasion *as touching the sense of it* is not always present. . . . (2) There may be divers degrees of this persuasion . . .' (Medulla Bk. 1, ch. 27, para. 19). Thus the difference in emphasis is circumstantial and the distinction in definition is largely academic and itself fades under the larger definitions of more seminal investigations: all sides agreed on the substance of the matter.

Was there then a further divide over a related matter, viz; how assurance is obtained/increased? It is rightly said that Calvin stressed our reliance on the promise and the character of God. The Puritans also stressed this above all else, but gave notable prominence to sanctification, godliness, as a further and essential ground of assurance. Again, the difference is not nearly so great as is sometimes supposed. First of all Calvin said that while the promises and character of God is the first and main ground of assurance and has exclusive pride of place, yet general sanctification and godliness has a vital and supportive role (*Inst.* Bk. 3, ch. 14 sectns. 18-20). On the other hand, the Puritans, while stressing the evidential value of sanctification and good works, roundly declared with Calvin that the prime place in assurance was to be given to the character and promises of God (see the passages from Bridge, Sharpe, Sibbes and Goodwin in my book *The Genius of Puritanism* pages: 82, 118, 119, 110; also the so-called 'legalistic' Ames: Medulla Bk. 1 ch. 30 paras. 13-15). Only after and under this was the evidential value of good works of value. Thus, once again, we have essential and wide unity among the Reformers and the Puritans.

As Calvin wrote (or was it Peter Martyr or Ames or Goodwin?): 'Conscience being thus founded, built up and established, is further established by the consideration of works, inasmuch as they are proofs of God dwelling in us. Since then, this confidence in works has no place unless you have previously fixed your whole confidence on the mercy of God, it should not seem contrary to that on which it depends. Wherefore, when we exclude confidence in works, we merely mean that the Christian mind must not turn back to the merit of works as an aid to salvation, but must dwell entirely on the free promise of justification. But we forbid no believer to confirm and support this faith by the signs of the divine favour towards him. For if when we call to mind the gifts which God has bestowed upon us, they are like rays of the divine countenance, by which we are enabled to behold the highest light of his goodness; much more is this the case with the gift of good works, which shows that we have received the Spirit of adoption' (*Inst.* Bk. 3, ch. 14, sectn. 18).

Yours warmly,

PETER LEWIS.

Chapter 14

Patience in Tribulation

As we have seen, Christian experience involves the feelings, emotions and affections of the soul. Attention has been devoted to the role of the moral law and its effects. Stress was laid on that subject first not only because it is neglected but because that is where our experience of the Gospel begins. Religion without the fear of God is spurious religion and the person who has never been convicted of sin should question whether he has ever been converted. Those who have experienced conviction of sin, have repented and believed, glory in that free justification which comes by faith in Christ. Joy because of justification is an experience. The love of God to us and our love to him is also experience. These experiences must not be set in conflict with each other. They are all important. Balance is necessary within the sphere of Christian experience. We should never lose sight of the essential unity of knowledge, experience and practice; head, heart and hands; faith, love and good works. These, held in proportion, make Christians to whom the Lord comes in his complacent love (John 14:23).

We like to think about experiences of joy, love and power, but trial and tribulation occupy a major part of what the Scriptures tell us about experience. Testimony meetings describing conversion we hear quite often. It is an encouragement to hear of those who tell us of their experience of free grace. We are accustomed to that. In some Pentecostal churches the emphasis is on Spirit-baptisms, tongues and healings. But whatever the character of the churches, how often is time allotted to share by hearing the testimony of those who have been brought through the deep waters of tribulation? Many can testify that they have learned more through adversity and trial than anything else.

Times of tribulation are intensely experimental. They are not joyous times. They are grievous, fainting times. But they are ordered for our profit and form an enriching part of our experience every bit as profitable as the 'power experiences' which seem to receive most of the attention and limelight. Without the experience of chastisement we are bastards and not sons (Heb. 12:8). Spoiled, deceived, arrogant, rascals and hypocrites we can easily be if there are no chastisement experiences.

With Scripture as a guide, let us examine the trial experiences more closely:

1. The experience of faith in suffering.
2. The experience of patience in tribulation.
3. The experience of desertion.
4. The experience of chastisement.

Because of the prominence which it has in Scripture, I would like to show how these factors are illustrated in the book of Job. So we have:

5. The experience of Job.

1. *The experience of faith in suffering*

Faith is the first and most important of all the graces wrought in us by God. Faith alone justifies. It is the grace which receives truth and by it all the other graces such as patience, love, meekness and hope are strengthened. Without faith all is lost. Without faith we cannot please God (Heb. 11:6). We are justified by faith and we live by the precious gift of faith which God has given us. Such faith has married us and joined us to Christ.

Peter tells us that our faith will be tried and tested (1 Pet. 1:7). We also know that God is faithful and will not allow us to be tried beyond our ability (1 Cor. 10:13). As Noah prepared for the great trial, and as Paul prepared himself in the face of great dangers and trials so that he could say, 'For I am ready not to be bound only, but also to die at Jerusalem for the name of the Lord Jesus' (Acts 21:13), so we must face up to experiences which involve suffering and experiences which undoubtedly will test our faith. We are 'heirs of God, and joint-heirs with Christ: if so be that we suffer with him' (Rom. 8:17).

The word suffer means to experience pain in soul or body. The word translated 'affliction' (*thlipsis*) in the New Testament is very expressive. It means pressure. To suffer affliction is to suffer pressure, or to be pressed down. The Hebrew word for afflict (*anah*) is also very expressive. It means to lower. Peter speaks of heaviness through many trials. We get the idea, then, of being brought low through pressures and weights being placed upon us. One could think of being pressed down and lowered into a pit or dungeon as was Jeremiah or George Wishart, the martyr at St. Andrews, in Scotland.

The word suffering is not far removed from the word tribulation used in our next main heading. Tribulation means straitness or distress (Hebrew: *tsarah*) but when we turn to the New Testament the word is synonymous with affliction (*thlipsis*). Tribulations or afflictions bring sufferings in their wake.

What do we regard as tribulations which bring sufferings? Are they reproach, strife, spoiling of goods and persecution leading perhaps to banishment and death? These comprise one form of tribulation. But we are by no means to confine tribulation to forces opposed to the Gospel. Innumerable troubles afflict all men and from these believers are by no means immune. Because he is spiritually sensitive, the believer can experience acute suffering or distress through temptations, adjustment problems, relationship trials, financial perplexities, frustrations, disappointments, oppressions at work or depressions at home. Unlike the unbeliever, the believer finds no relief or pleasure in fleshly or worldly means to relieve those pressures and trials which he experiences. He may indulge in lawful recreations but he knows that these offer no solution to his sufferings. The invitation from the world to eat, drink and be merry and to forget is hollow mockery to the Christian. Stoicism on the one hand or 'drowning his sorrows' on the other are no solutions. Reliance or trust in God for the Christian is imperative. He must lean upon the means of grace for his faith to be sustained.

It is here that we must distinguish very clearly between faith and experience. A dangerous division seems to be developing among believers. There are those who live by their experience and those who stress doctrine and faith. One Baptist minister has gone so far as to say that we do not need the Word since by supernatural gifts we have direct access to God by the Spirit.

We have been examining the words tribulation, affliction and suffering. When we are pressed down and lowered in spirit, when we are troubled on every side, fightings without and fears within, when our more exalted and encouraging experiences of joy and victory disappear, then we are left with faith alone alongside the Word of God. Gone then is the thrill of the marching band, gone is the voice of song, gone is the aura of excitement and fellowship. The believer is alone. Behind him and before him are adversaries bent on his destruction. The last thing he *feels* like doing is fighting, but fight the good fight of faith he must. He has no joy, only pain. What else does he have? He has faith and the armour of God. And what is the armour of God? If we analyse Ephesians chapter six, verses fourteen to seventeen we shall see that the armour of God is not experiences but doctrine, and the only way the armour is made to work is by faith. All the items of the armour have to do with truth (shoes, dress, breastplate, shield, sword and helmet). Faith in these various doctrines or truths is the only way in which they will function. A man may go to battle without any feelings of joy, power or blessing and yet fight as well as he has ever fought as he exercises the knowledge that goes with his faith. In other words, it is a well-taught and well-experienced faith that sees him through, not the memories of happy times he may have had. We should be concentrating on preparation for war, not spending our energy on sensations and excitements.

Our concern, our prayer and our efforts are to this end that the Reformed Faith be revived in the world and that this faith of our fathers triumph over everything else. Why? Well, to us that is the triumph of the Word of God. Our priority is preaching and teaching. Exposition, counsel, advice and exhortation from the Word are to this end, that faith may be nurtured, strengthened, built up and made victorious. Experience is vital and important. We neglect it at our peril but it comes after faith. If experience usurps the central place which we give to the Word of God, then experience will become a substitute for study and preaching. That is exactly what we are seeing with some ministers. They have succumbed to the miserable deception that experience will do all the work. Sensations will draw the people and charismatic excitement will keep them happy. We hear complaints from believers that they are no longer fed with expository preaching. Gone is the labour, care and discipline essential for the feeding of the flock. Gone is a comprehensive command of the grand doctrines of the Bible which engender the obedience of faith and build up strong, resilient, mature Christians. Instead of a hearty meal for hungry souls we have pop-corn and fizzy drinks, peanuts and marshmallows, coloured balloons, vain repetitions, and a general overall emphasis on entertainment.

Let the trumpet sound for a return to the centrality of the Word, the doctrines, the teachings and the truths of sovereign grace which alone will build up the sheep and the lambs, enabling and preparing them for days of trial and testing. A minister who ceases to labour in doctrine should retire immediately from service (1 Tim. 5:17). Old cliches and stale anecdotes will never feed the flock. Nor can a narrative of experiences replace the ministry of the Word.

Trial and testing of faith are inevitable. From time to time we see professors who have relied on experiences, and who have no heart for trial or difficulty, falling away. In the parable of the sower, our Lord gives a warning that there will be those who endure for a little while but when tribulation or persecution arise they are offended and fall away. In our Western society we could profitably suggest the word 'inconvenience'. When inconveniences arise they are offended. The forsaking of ease and worldly pleasures for the discipline of worship is too high a price to pay! The assertion of family discipline and the requirements needful for faithful attendance at the sanctuary are deemed inconvenient. When challenged about their neglect of God's house and God's people, fruitless professors talk about what they used to do and the experiences they once had, but they deceive themselves. Faith, except it produce good works, is dead (Jas. 2:14-20). A faith which refuses to suffer inconvenience is no faith, as our Lord said: 'Whosoever he be of you that forsaketh not all that he hath, he cannot be my disciple' (Luke 14:33).

There is experience which might be called the experience of notion or idea. This is an experience that is devoid of reality. It is the experience of the temporary believer who has joy for a while but then, when the reality of suffering inconvenience for Christ's sake presses upon him, he either falls away or takes up the posture of resting on a profession made some time in the past. Fair words and speeches about experience are meaningless unless backed up by daily works of righteousness which spring from faith and prove that faith to be God-given.

2. *The experience of patience in tribulation*

Having laid stress upon the importance of faith and the Word of God alone during times of trial or suffering, it is important that we do not lose sight of the sovereignty of the Holy Spirit in his direct operations upon the soul when a Bible may not be in sight. I know that this may seem to contradict the emphasis that has been made on study, and so on, but we must not lose the balance. There are times of exceptional trial or sorrow when the Holy Spirit works in an exceptional way. During such times extraordinary comfort, help and support are given. Distress may be intense and the sufferer may be too distracted to be able to concentrate. He may be unable to pray and if he prays at all it is with groanings that cannot be uttered. Then it is that he is upheld and passages which he has learned are brought back to mind. Often an inexpressible peace is inwardly imparted and an assurance and joy given. Some believers have afterwards described such a trial as the most outstanding spiritual experience of their lives. That the Lord acts in this exceptional way has the support of Scripture. He says: 'When thou passest through the waters, I will be with thee; and through the rivers, they shall not overflow thee: when thou walkest through the fire, thou shalt not be burned; neither shall the flame kindle upon thee' (Isa. 43:2. See also Isa. 41:10,14; Ps. 66:10-12; 91:15; Amos 9:9; Matt. 7:25; 2 Tim. 4:17,18).

This experience of comfort is one of inward strengthening as though a secret power was being placed within, an army of soldiers entering in to garrison the fortress of the soul. The word 'patience', to which we have become accustomed in the Authorized Version, expresses this inward strengthening very well. It means the same as endurance. Patience gives the idea of a passive quality and in that sense it is misleading, because this word endurance (*hupomone*) has an active meaning to it. It conveys the meaning of strength or power to continue, persevere or carry on. This patience, or endurance, is a power imparted by the Holy Spirit by which he gives perseverance and victory. Patience or endurance in trials or in one particular trial can be experienced in a constant way throughout a lifetime or be an extraordinary experience for a believer during a short time of particular affliction.

This patience or endurance can rise to an experience of rejoicing. Paul, in explaining this, reasons in a circular fashion. Trials are used by God to produce endurance (patience). The possession of endurance furnishes experience or proof that our hope of eternal glory is not empty and vain (Rom. 5:2-4). This proof causes rejoicing in the glory of God and the rejoicing in turn increases our endurance so that we arrive where we started. Note that Paul refers to trials rather than experiences of power or joy as providing proof of the reality of our hope of eternal glory.

The experience of the Holy Spirit in the heart to give endurance enables believers to be consistent. Thomas Manton suggests that this endurance or patience can be seen in three ways. There is, he says, a bearing patience, a waiting patience and a working patience. A *bearing* patience is that constancy in adversity when we face up to our trials without murmurings. It requires this bearing patience to endure the evils of this world after which we shall inherit the promise (Heb. 6:12).

A *waiting* patience is that quiet endurance which continues until it is God's good pleasure to turn the tide of tribulation away from us and refresh us. If that is not to be, then it is to endure the trial with patience until the race of life is over.

A *working* patience is when we perpetually apply ourselves to our responsibilities with self-denying obedience combatting weariness, disordered thoughts, a troubled conscience, temptations, dreariness, distractions and sluggishness.

The work of comfort forms an important part of the ministry (2 Cor. 1:3-7). The skilful pastor will not only diagnose correctly but, as a wise physician, will be competent in the application of the balm of Gilead. He will be skilful in drawing material and arguments from all parts of Scripture, but particularly the Psalms. The ministry of comfort requires a high degree of discernment and a scrupulous eye for detail in the area of God's providence – especially in the observation that those things which seem most adverse and painful are for good and often prove to be for the highest good of the believer.

Consolation can always be derived from a consideration of Paul's contrast between things temporal and things spiritual and the relative lightness of our present affliction compared with the glory to come (2 Cor. 4:16-5:6). It is often surprising to find that unusual subjects such as the gentleness and compassion of Christ in his ministry (Isa. 41:1-4), strengthen the believer in tribulation.

Passages in the Song of Solomon are often referred to to illustrate aspects and reasons for desertion (S. of S. 3:1-4; 5:1-8).

To distinguish between different trial experiences is of the utmost importance. This is where Job's comforters failed lamentably. A

rebellious believer under temptation may not need comfort at all
but rather reproof which should be faithfully administered.   One
suffering from a desertion experience or depression (melancholy)
needs the most gentle and patient treatment and to that matter we
now turn.

3. *The experience of desertion*

Suppose the believer comes into many trials together or enters one
particular grievous and painful trial and finds that the empowering
and comforting blessings of the Holy Spirit are absent.   Suppose he
discovers himself in a new situation; the shattering experience of
desertion!   Is he then to conclude that he is not a child of God after
all?   Is not the desertion he experiences proof that he has been
deceived as to his standing in grace and he is a reprobate after all?
By no means!   The Scriptures make provision for this experience.
The condition commonly allied to it is depression.   'Why art thou
cast down O my soul? and why art thou disquieted in me?' (Ps. 42:
11).   'My tears have been my meat day and night, while they
continually say unto me, Where is thy God?' (Ps. 42:3).   'Thou didst
hide thy face, and I was troubled' (Ps. 30:7).
    Other passages speak in more vivid terms: 'Fearfulness and
trembling are come upon me, and horror hath overwhelmed me'
(Ps. 55:5).   Remember, too, that the psalms we rightly call messian-
ic and take as the very words of Christ (spoken hundreds of years
before the time by inspiration of the Holy Spirit), were also the
actual living experience of the writers.   Hence, when David cries,
'my God, my God, why hast thou forsaken me?', he is describing an
experience of desertion (Ps. 22:1).   Again, when he prays, 'hide
not thy face from me' (Ps. 69:17; Ps. 143:7), he knows all too well
the reality of being alone.   How can we reconcile this to Hebrews
thirteen, verses five and six: 'And be content with such things as
ye have: for he hath said, I will never leave thee, nor forsake thee.
So that we may boldly say, The Lord is my helper, and I will not
fear what man shall do unto me'?   It is true that God will never
forsake his children either in his providential dealings with them or
with regard to the Holy Spirit whom he has given to dwell in them

for ever. This, however, does not contradict the fact that for sovereign reasons of his own he will withdraw his presence and diminish the help he affords, chastise the believer and for wise reasons cause him to go through severe trials.

One of the main lessons from the book of Job is that God does not provide explanations. With Job we are left to draw our own conclusions. Instead of explanations God causes his glory to pass before the wondering gaze of Job. God may permit this experience to develop the faith and spiritual fibre of a Christian, or to increase his humility and dependence, or to bring him into a much greater sense of spiritual realities and appreciation of the love of the Redeemer. In this connection the Puritans often quoted Song of Solomon chapter five verse six: 'But my beloved had withdrawn himself, and was gone: my soul failed when he spake: I sought him . . . but he gave me no answer'. The love and presence of Christ is appreciated most by those who have been sorely tried on the road to the new Jerusalem.

In the experience of desertion, spiritual barrenness or depression, allowances must be made both for distorted thinking in the mind because of strain and sorrow and for the malice of Satan ever ready to exploit to the full any situation of weakness in the believer. He will propose a wrong use of Scripture texts, will distort spiritual principles, encourage despair and attempt to inflame the conscience in a wrong way. His objectives will also include the destruction of faith and the inciting of murmuring and rebellion. That believers should understand these stratagems and the nature of the battle is much to their advantage, and when they come through such times it is to the honour and praise of God.

4. *The experience of chastisement*

As we have seen, there are various reasons why desertion is permitted. To bring correction may be a main or a supplementary reason behind desertion and if this is so then the desertion can be regarded as a chastisement. Believers are never punished in a retributive sense, because they have been punished already for all their sins in the person of Christ their head.   Yet they are punished or chastised for their disobedience and sinfulness with correction in view.

A vast amount of correction is required in every redeemed sinner. By the means of grace, especially preaching, by the correction provided through teaching, by the example of consistent believers and by the reproof and instruction of the elders, this work of correction is carried on.   Chastisement by way of temporal and spiritual trials forms part of the experience of every believer.   If a person is without such correction then he is illegitimate, a bastard and not a true-born son! (Heb. 12:8).   Correction is essential and therefore inevitable.   It is a non-joyful experience, one which can be very painful.   In different ways God exposes the hatefulness, pride, self-will, foolish and unworthy thinking, carelessness, impurity, disobedience, slackness, lack of discipline, unspirituality, covetousness, lies, hypocrisy, resentment, false imaginings about others and other sins that remain within our hearts.   He has many ways of humbling his children.   He has wonderful ways, too, of humbling preachers. Once let a preacher think that he is eloquent or able of himself and God will soon show him what a pompous fool he has become.   This he may do by deserting the preacher or taking his memory from him when he needs it most, so that he flounders in mid-air.   (Reader, we do not know how God is correcting others, so if your preacher falters it would perhaps be better to wonder if poor listeners or sleepers are not the cause!)   The ways in which God corrects his children are countless.

Chastisements may be prolonged and endurance is needed to weather them.   Two temptations predominate in the chastisement experience.   The first is to despise the chastening, that is, to rebel against it.   The second is to faint under the rebuke of chastening, that is, to become listless, despairing, sulky and neglectful of our active responsibilities.   To faint is to be prostrate and often those chastised begin to neglect the very means of their restoration, namely, the prayer meeting and the services of worship.

The principal passage dealing with chastisement is Hebrews chapter twelve verses four to eleven.   But there are others eloquent with instruction such as Psalm seventy-three.   The psalmist declares that he had been plagued all the day long and chastened every morning.   The reason for this was distorted thinking or error. When corrected, the psalmist confesses his ignorance and folly. He had been thinking like an idiot and is grieved that he had behaved in a beastly way before God.

Though painful, we are assured that chastisements afterwards yield the peaceable fruit of righteousness. When we have been chastised, we are less critical and harsh and more gentle and patient with others. Chastisement convinces the believer of his own deceitfulness, pride and inward corruption. Chastisement strengthens faith inasmuch as it leads to greater dependence upon God and upon the promises of Scripture. Correction leaves the Christian wiser and more submissive. The painful experience of chastisement causes him to value heaven more and esteem the inheritance laid up for him there, and to think less of earthly possessions and comforts.

5. *The experience of Job*

That the canon of Scripture should include such an extraordinary book as that of Job should fill us with wonder and gratitude. All the experiences to which reference has been made seem to unite in Job.

There was none like him, a green, fruitful, beautiful tree planted by the rivers of plenty; just, upright, careful, humble and consistent – none like Job, a choice saint indeed! God is never the author of evil. He permits evil and Satan is allowed to strip the tree of all its prosperity, taking from Job even the fruit of his loins. To lose one child is exceedingly grievous. To lose all in a stroke, who can bear? Job is shaken to the core (Job 1:20) but retains his faith and blesses God. Amazing! Meanwhile the malice of Satan knows no limits. At the next assembly of heaven Job is vindicated, but present is Satan once more. This advocate of malice makes fresh accusations and applies for a fresh trial of Job's faith, this time being permitted to make a savage personal attack, like the onslaught of a hailstorm upon a tree leaving it bleak and white. Job is smitten from top to toe with unsightly, agonizing, humiliating boils. Even his wife abhors him, bidding him to curse God and die! The naked tree is shaken in the wind. Job curses not God but the day he was born (Job 3:3). Nor are his trials at an end. We are gregarious creatures by nature and the friendship, goodwill, comfort, help, gifts and support of our circle of friends both near and far mean more to us than we are prone to realise. It was so with Job, but instead of comforting him, his friends tormented him. The tree, now a bare skeleton, was blasted with three rounds of hail and sleet and finally by an ice-blizzard from Elihu which left Job speechless. Yet all the while the roots of faith were wrapping ever more tightly round the 'Rock of Ages'.

If we review the headings of our consideration of tribulation we will see that Job endured the whole range of painful experiences, 1. The trial of his faith through prolonged and varied sufferings. 2. The exercise of patience and endurance under terrible tribulation. 3. Desertion by God, and 4. Chastisement and correction.

It may be that the most bitter of Job's sufferings came as a result of the superficial theories of his friends who did not succeed in their attempts to deduce a satisfactory doctrine of providence. Job was more than a match for them, but their charges stung him sharply and increased the pain of his mind, the varying processes of which are opened to view in detail. For an example of the most cruel and unjust accusations against Job read the twenty-second chapter verses five to ten. What patience did the sufferer show under the preposterous charges of extortion, robbery, violence and wilful contempt of the fatherless and widows!

Through all his winter's night of woe Job's faith remained intact. Sound theology is not to be despised. A strong faith feeds on meat (Heb. 5:14). Job's faith creaked under the strain of colossal pressure but did not snap. In his anguish he cried, 'though he slay me, yet will I trust in him' (Job 13:15). His faith was stronger at the end of his tribulations than at the beginning. The experience and the exercise of reason, argument and counter-argument, contributed further to the stature of Job as a man of faith.

What of Job's endurance? He did not lack in giving eloquent expression to his impatience. Yet in the New Testament the Holy Spirit refers only to his patience (Jas. 5:10). In his experience he plaintively rehearsed his case before God. 'I will say unto God, Do not condemn me; shew me wherefore thou contendest with me' (Job 10:2). Job's example shows us that it is good to open our hearts to God in our troubles. This is better than smothering our griefs or adopting an attitude of stoicism. Similarly, Jeremiah in his anguish vented his feelings to the Almighty and expressed his resolution not to preach any more (Jer. 20:9). God's gentleness made the prophet great, for he supported Jeremiah and made the Word to burn in his bones bringing his resolution to nothing. Likewise Job was supported, being able to endure his trials.

This brings us to the subject of Job's desertion. Undoubtedly the loss of God's felt favour outweighed all other elements in the balance of Job's grief. 'Oh that I knew where I might find him!' he cries (Job 23:3). If we liken the verbal trouncings meted out by Job's friends to gusts of sleet, then the absence of God's felt presence and approbation was none other than the long bitter winter itself. This desertion was not merely passive in the sense that God was removed and silent, but active in the sense that Job felt that God was fighting actively against him. 'He teareth me in his wrath' (see Job 16:9).

Job's restoration to peace and blessedness did not come by debates, conferences and speculations. God himself, by his immediate presence, power and glory alone, brought to an end the most profound of all Job's sufferings. Although reproved, the sufferer was restored to deep contentment and happiness. If God was with him who could be against him? The ice of desertion and the frost of adversity melted away. The spring of a restored communion brought healing and renewal in all departments.

Job makes sacrifices for his erring friends, whereupon his boils are replaced by the bloom of renewed health. God has returned. The sun of a new day of prosperity and joy is upon the horizon.

It would not be far wrong to call the book of Job the book of repentance or the book of advanced sanctification. If the subject of desertion prevails, the question of chastisement does so no less. His chastisement was grievous but led to correction and repentance. God's servant at the commencement of his trial was already far advanced in the school of sanctification. The experience brought much to the surface that needed to be repented of. The sufferer himself testified that his experience before compared with what came after was as hearing is compared with sight. 'I have heard of thee by the hearing of the ear: but now mine eye seeth thee. Wherefore I abhor myself, and repent in dust and ashes' (Job 42:5,6).

The chastisement which had made feeble the knees of Job resulted in his correction. He had been guilty of contending with his Maker and of attempting to instruct the Omnipotent. Of this he repents. 'Behold, I am vile; what shall I answer thee? I will lay mine hand upon my mouth. Once have I spoken; but I will not answer: yea, twice; but I will proceed no further' (Job 40:4,5).

Conclusions

Adequate evidence has been presented to show the prominence in Scripture of those experiences which are painful but which fulfil a major role in our lives. Failure to understand and interpret these experiences has led to incompetence in counselling troubled souls.

Without adequate analysis and without spiritual consideration the perplexed and the tried are chided for not claiming the victory. Moreover, those who have imbibed the philosophy that Christianity consists entirely of felt experiences of joy, power, miracles and sensations have become by this error extremely vulnerable and ill-equipped to stand in days of tribulation.

The remedy is to strive constantly for a full intellectual, practical and experimental grasp of the Scriptures. Man shall not live by bread alone but by every word that proceeds out of the mouth of God (Deut. 8:3).

Chapter 15

The Baptism of the Spirit

WE have seen that the realm of spiritual experience is broad. Experiences are diverse. We cannot afford to neglect any aspect; nor should we allow one kind of experience to be exalted at the expense of others. We have seen humiliation because of sin to be essential. Joy because of justification and love because of adoption form main pillars in the temple of Christian experience. Of necessity believers go through times of trial and chastisement when they learn much and advance on the road to conformity to Christ, which we call sanctification. The rôle of the person of the Holy Spirit in experience is, of course, central to all Christian experience. We come now to consider the Holy Spirit's work as follows:

1. In regeneration.
2. In filling individuals.
3. In baptising the Church.

1. *In regeneration*

God the Holy Spirit is the agent (the one who executes or performs a work) of the creation of the world. He is the author of the Scriptures. He inspired the prophets of old. That Christ was conceived by the virgin Mary was of the Holy Spirit (Luke 1:35) and he anointed our Lord for his ministry. He was also the one through whom Christ gave himself as an offering for sin. He raised our Lord from the dead. The creation and the resurrection were Trinitarian acts inasmuch as the three persons of the Trinity acted in concert, but the Holy Spirit was the immediate agent in those acts of power (Rom. 1:4).

In the forming of the Church, the Holy Spirit's special work is regeneration and sanctification. Election, predestination, calling, justification and glorification are designated to the Father (Rom. 8:28 ff.). Christ's work was to become our righteousness through his life on earth and our redemption through his death on the cross. His present work is to intercede for us at the right hand of God and to work in the application of redemption. The Spirit's major work is to regenerate and sanctify the elect of God.

An understanding of regeneration is important, not only because of the foremost place it has in salvation but also because so many talk today of the baptism of the Spirit as though it were a second regeneration. The idea that prevails is that there is first the conversion experience and then some time after that it is necessary for a Christian to have a second experience in which something happens to him so that he is never the same again – a kind of second regeneration is supposed to take place. So there is the notion that you have second-rate or half-regenerated Christians and first-rate, wholly-regenerated Christians. Oft-repeated stories of the experiences of Charles Finney and D. L. Moody, plus the account of what happened when Paul was at Ephesus (Acts 19:2) are frequently cited to support what is a totally confused and unscriptural idea.

That every Christian is regenerated or born again once and once only is fundamental. When born again he is wholly born, not half-born, but wholly for time and for eternity. The analogy of birth holds good in that as the babe grows and develops so the believer born of God grows and makes progress. Where there is spiritual birth there is spiritual life and if there is no spiritual life it is because there has never been spiritual birth. 'That which is born of the flesh is flesh; and that which is born of the Spirit is spirit' (John 3:6). The force of our Lord's words to Nicodemus is unmistakable. He is asserting the reality of spiritual life once it is born in an individual in contrast to the fleshly life of the unregenerate. This regeneration is referred to in different ways. It is called a quickening together with Christ from spiritual death (Eph. 2:5); the dead hearing and believing to eternal life (John 5:24,25); a resurrection of power by God from the dead (Eph. 1:19,20); a new birth by God's will (Jas. 1:18; 1 Pet. 1:3). It is referred to also as a baptism. 'For by one Spirit we are all baptized into one body' (1 Cor. 12:13).

The word baptism is an expressive word not to be deprived of its potency. It means to immerse, to dip, to submerge. During the whole life of the Greek language it has had this unvarying meaning.[1] It is a word used to convey the meaning of immersion or submerging and the concept is that which is total and radical, complete and final. That is the sense in which John the Baptist, our Lord and his apostles used the term.

When we are baptised into Christ we are made one with Christ and that act of the Holy Ghost is an act which is total and final. We have been baptized into Christ, sunk into him, amalgamated with him. We have not been sprinkled into him. Baptism into Christ or regeneration is radical. It is to be raised from the dead with him. It is a new birth. Believers have, by this regenerating act, been made one with Christ in his death and resurrection. We have been baptised in and by the Spirit.[2] If a person has not been baptised in the Spirit and by the Spirit into Christ then he is outside of Christ and still in his sins. Every believer without exception has been baptised into Christ by the Spirit.[2] (If the reader is confused by the prepositions used: *in* the Spirit and *by* the Spirit, please refer to the footnote at this point.)

This spiritual baptism is referred to by Paul when he declares: 'For as many of you as have been baptised into Christ have put on Christ' (Gal. 3:27). How could it be otherwise but that those joined to Christ have his life? He continues to assert that all believers, irrespective of any human distinctions whatsoever, are thereby 'one in Christ' (Gal. 3:28). Likewise to the Romans Paul puts the fundamental question, Don't you know that so many of us as were baptised into Jesus Christ were baptised into his death? He concludes that we were therefore buried with him by baptism into death; that like as Christ was raised up from the dead by the glory of the Father, even so we also should walk in newness of life (Rom. 6:3,4). The great majority of commentators take baptism in Romans 6:3,4 to mean 'water baptism'—Calvin, Lange, Lightfoot, Shedd, Hodge, Vincent, Haldane, Barnes and John Murray to name just a few. Water baptism is the symbol of Spirit baptism since it approximates so closely and depicts so accurately the union with Christ effected in spiritual baptism. The consensus of expository opinion is right therefore in taking Romans 6:3,4 to refer to water baptism as the symbol of union with Christ in his death, burial and resurrection. Is it possible for two things to be spoken of together, the symbol and the reality? The answer surely is, yes! For instance when we speak of the cup we mean two things at the same time—the cup which contains the literal wine as a symbol, and communion with Christ which is an invisible but nonetheless living reality—not the one nor the other, but both together (1 Cor. 12:16, 17).

When Paul speaks of 'one Lord, one faith, one baptism', to the Ephesians, that momentous initiation of all believers into one Lord by means of the one faith is indicated. This spiritual baptism, our initiation into Christ, is visibly and symbolically portrayed by water baptism which our Lord has commanded and which is thus obligatory for all believers (Mark 16:16; Matt. 28:18-20; Acts 2:38). The amazing reality of spiritual union with Christ in his death and resurrection is perfectly expressed in the ordinance of baptism by burial in water. The burial simultaneously points to the death and resurrection of Christ by which the believer is identified with God, not partially nor half-heartedly but totally and radically. By the death of Christ (which he himself referred to as a baptism, Mark 10:39) all the believer's sins are washed away for ever. The believer is justified by faith. Justification is never partial. It is one hundred per cent. By virtue of union with Christ the believer now has the life of Christ—and hence is to walk in newness of life. He does not possess half of Christ or a quarter, to receive the other part later. In regeneration he is united to the whole of Christ by the Holy Spirit. He does not have a little part of the Holy Spirit, to receive a great part later. He has the Holy Spirit as an indwelling person—not part, but all of the Holy Spirit as a person in him to carry on the work of conformity to Christ which will continue throughout his earthly pilgrimage.

Regeneration produces faith (John 1:12,13) and faith joins the believer to Christ. The believer is married to Christ (Jer. 3:14; John 17:23; 15:4) and by marriage to Christ is married to God. Water-immersion, therefore, is the sign and seal of what has already taken place in the Spirit.

What effect does this baptism into Christ have upon a person's experience? Paul tells us, 'If any man be in Christ, he is a new creature: old things have passed away: behold all things are become new.' On the day of writing this I interviewed a man requesting baptism and church membership. He believes he was born again in a public house. The change was such that he instantly left his beer mug, half-filled, and never returned. Such was the change that he forgot all about his bicycle which he had left outside. After fourteen days he remembered it, went back and to his amazement found it untouched! He had been wholly taken up with a new life. All things became new—thoughts, affections, language and actions. All things became *new*—but not perfect.

Justification is perfect but the sanctification that follows is a process and involves progress. Perfect holiness is never attained in this life. This newness of life consists of *a walk*. A whole supply of energy and life is required for walking from one year to the next. In the spiritual life a world of spiritual supply is required and this the Holy Spirit does impart from the moment of new birth. It is not as though the Spirit by one immense operation either at the moment of birth or in a later experience so affects a believer that he is perfect and glorified. That will come only at the time of resurrection at the end of the world. The spiritual life is a moment-by-moment, day-to-day experience. Our Lord promised that the Holy Spirit would be in us (John 14:17) – 'He shall be in you' – not an influence merely – but as a person, as God in the whole of his personality, he will be in you!

To what measure is he in all believers? We consider now the subject of the filling of the Spirit.

2. *In filling individuals*

The Holy Spirit regenerates us, seals us, anoints us, communes with us, assures us, enables us, sanctifies us and fills us. All these aspects are different and wherever distinctions are indicated in Scripture it is important for us to observe these distinctive features.

Regeneration takes place in an instant, in a moment or in the twinkling of an eye. With regeneration comes sealing and anointing. Sealing has to do with assurance and anointing with understanding. Since both sealing and anointing are often confused with the idea of a personal baptism of the Spirit it will be helpful to comment on these aspects of the Holy Spirit's work.

Sealing

A seal is a stamp or impression stamped upon an object to indicate ownership and authentication of possession, the seal bearing the distinctive crest or insignia of the owner. The lineaments or character of Christ have been stamped or sealed upon and within the believer. In the new nature he has been made after the likeness of Christ.   The old man (Col. 3:9) is gone for ever.   A sealed person can never again be unregenerate.   The fleshly and carnal elements (Rom. 7:13-25; Gal. 5:17) remain, a subject which is expounded in a separate chapter, but the new man is sealed by God with a seal of ownership or adoption.   The foundation of God standeth sure, having this seal, the Lord knoweth them that are his (2 Tim. 2:19). He knows his own and the angels know them (Luke 15:10).   If the seals of the Medes and Persians were respected and not to be tampered with, how much more the seal of God, the seal which bears his image![3] The sealing itself is neither metaphorical nor external.   It is a sealing with the Holy Spirit of God.   It is a stamping of the divine character upon the human personality.   It is a fresh and indestructible communication to the believer of the image of God which was defaced through the fall (see Philip Hughes on 2 Cor. 3:18).   We received the Spirit by hearing with faith (Col. 3:2) and by believing we received the seal or impress of the Spirit in our hearts – 'believing ye were sealed' (Eph. 1:13).[4]   Grieve not the Holy Spirit by whom you were sealed, says Paul (Eph. 4:20).   In other words, do not act in a way which contradicts the nature of Christ with whose image you have been sealed.

There seems to be unnecessary division over this matter of the sealing.   I said that sealing has to do with assurance.   This is indicated in 2 Corinthians 1:21,22.   'Now he which stablisheth us with you in Christ, and hath anointed us, is God; Who hath also sealed us, and given us the earnest of the Spirit in our hearts.'   Here the establishing or making firm of believers is in view and to this end the believer has received an enlightenment or anointing, a discernment to understand teaching, and having been sealed[5] has been given the Holy Spirit as the earnest or guarantee in his heart that he will come into his full inheritance in glory.   The seal is an inward image of God upon the regenerate, not to be confused with 'the earnest' who is the Holy Spirit himself, who bears witness to the believer that in fact he is a child of God and that, having been sealed with God's image, he continues always to have that seal or image.

This leads to the whole realm of subjective experience.   As justification is always the basis of sanctification, so the seal of God, witnessed to by the Holy Spirit, is the basis of assurance.   Not what we have done but what *he* has done in uniting us to Christ is the ground of our assurance.   Having sealed us, the Holy Spirit bears direct witness to that sealing (Rom. 8:16; 1 John 4:13) – that is, he assures us that we are made after the image of Christ.   If we understand sealing in this way, then testimonies to sealing experiences make sense.   If we take the view that some are sealed at regeneration when they believe and others in later experiences we will have two classes of Christians, sealed and not sealed, whereas in Ephesians chapter one the apostle is speaking of one class of Christians from first to last.

Objectively, that is viewed from the throne of God, all believers are sealed by the Spirit in regeneration.   At this time they become new creations or new creatures.   No such new creation is without God's signature or seal.   The seal can be viewed objectively in this way, but then there is the subjective realisation by the believer of that seal.   The strength with which such realisation is experienced varies tremendously.   With some it is very powerful.   To others, who may be inhibited for one reason or another, the seal can be obscure.   This obscurity can pertain with respect to both its meaning as well as the feeling of assurance.   This matter can be illustrated with the case of Thomas.   Our Lord had been raised from the dead as certainly for Thomas as for the other disciples.   Thomas's perception and assurance of that was for a time very obscure but it became certain and clear.

It is certainly true that some Christians have a full assurance of salvation (Heb. 6:11) and some do not, such assurance being something which all believers should be diligent to obtain.   Subjective realisation of God's seal is stronger in some believers than others.

Unnecessary arguments and divisions arise among Christians when one aspect of truth is separated and divided from another.   For instance, there are some who stress the new birth and the sealing of the Spirit in such a way that no room is left for the outworking of the experience of these matters.   Conversion is the experimental aspect or other side of the coin of new birth.   Assurance is the experimental outworking of sealing.

The Holy Spirit, who is 'the earnest' or guarantee of our salvation, pledges to us that we are in Christ and that we are children by adoption, and that the promises are ours as well as the right to approach the throne of God with boldness (Heb. 4:14-16).

When Thomas Goodwin says we should sue God for the sealing of the Spirit is this right? Declares Goodwin: 'There is a promise of the Holy Ghost to come and fill your hearts with joy unspeakable and glorious, to seal you up to the day of redemption.   Sue this promise out, wait for it, rest not in believing only, rest not in assurances by graces only; there is a further assurance to be had.'[6]   That is a heartwarming, stirring exhortation and, provided it is understood in the sense of the Holy Spirit coming with power to confirm our sealing to us, it is first rate, for this subject is essentially ongoing and experimental. The new birth is the watershed. A river of experience flows thereafter.

The situation sometimes arises in counselling in which a believer lacks assurance. Others can see the marks and evidences of the new birth, but the person in question feels distressed by a lack of the direct witness of the Holy Spirit. Others can see a sealing but the person in question cannot. He is to be urged to beseech God for it.

Anointing

Paul, in referring to the establishing action of God whereby believers are made firm, refers to anointing, sealing and the earnest of the Spirit. All believers are anointed, sealed and given the earnest of the Spirit (cf. footnotes 4 and 5).

How do these works of the Spirit minister toward the establishment of believers? The anointing is described by John as an enlightenment given to believers whereby they are enabled to discern the teachings of Christ in contrast with the doctrines of antichrist (1 John 2:20,27 and 5:20). With regard to antichrists, John is saying in effect that we do not need these vagrant heretics to teach us because we have an anointing which they do not have and by that anointing we are able to discern all things relative to the divinity of Christ and our salvation in him as the only Son of God manifested in the flesh. This applies to Jehovah's Witness and Mormon cults today. The true believer discerns the anti-Christ nature of the heresies.

Filling

John the Baptist, Elizabeth and Zacharias were all filled with the Spirit, John for the ministry and Elizabeth and Zacharias to prophesy. At Pentecost the disciples were all filled with the Holy Spirit as were later (Acts 4:32) Stephen and Barnabas, men 'full of the Holy Ghost'. Paul was filled with the Holy Spirit (Acts 9:17 and 13:9). It might be said that being filled with the Spirit results in the development of Christian character as a whole and glorifies God by producing a consistent Christian testimony. Thus in Ephesians 5:18 being filled with the Spirit is spoken of in the same context as submission to others, thankfulness and joyfulness expressed in the singing of psalms, hymns and spiritual songs. Obviously there is an ebb and flow in the believer's experience of the Spirit. Also the

Holy Spirit fills believers for specific reasons such as enduing with power to preach, endurance to suffer, and so on.

The term 'filled' is a general one denoting the heightening of a believer's experience, the raising of his understanding, the endearing of his affections, the empowering of his will and the warming of his perceptions enabling him to appreciate fellowship with fellow believers and giving him delight in the worship of God. The filling of the Spirit is common to all believers. It is not the prerogative of an elite few; nor does the filling of the Spirit depend on any former special experience.

Moreover, the filling of the Spirit does not depend on possession of spiritual gifts. Some distinguish between temporary gifts and permanent gifts. Apostleship, prophecy, healing (that is, direct, immediate healing), miracle-working, discerning of spirits and tongues (Acts 2 and 1 Cor. 12:12-14) can be regarded as temporary. The word of wisdom, the word of knowledge, teaching, helps and administration, evangelism, the pastorate and faith can be regarded as permanent. Some might place the word of wisdom in the category of the extraordinary but it certainly helps to distinguish between that which is ordinary and permanent.

An example of distinguishing between the extraordinary and ordinary gifts is found in the Association records of Particular Baptists as long ago as 1656 in which a precise distinction was made as to what ceased with the apostles, namely, apostles, prophets, evangelists, gifts of healing, diversities of tongues, and what continued; namely, pastors, teachers, helps or those who rule, these three called elders whose joint office is to care for the church. Thereafter follows a list of duties including visiting the sick according to James 5:14.

How are we to explain the case of miserable believers who by their own admission are not filled with the Spirit and who may claim that they have never been filled with the Spirit? There are several explanations. One is that of temperament. Another is a lack of teaching. Yet another is a neglect of the means of grace. Yet another is grieving the Spirit.

We have been speaking of individuals. What about churches? Churches as a whole can decline into a lukewarm condition like the church of Laodicea. On the other hand a church or churches can be in a healthy state being edified by the Holy Spirit. This brings us to consider Pentecost and the baptism of the Church with the Holy Spirit.

3. *In baptising the Church*

When John the Baptist declared that he baptised with water unto repentance, but one was coming after him who would baptise with the Holy Ghost and fire he was pointing to the exaltation and Godhead of Jesus Christ. As God he would send the Holy Spirit into the world in a new way. The fulfilment at Pentecost of John's prediction marked the birthday of the Spirit into the world, just as Jesus' birth at Bethlehem marked Jesus' birth into the world. This is not to say that our Lord and the Holy Spirit were not both active in Old Testament times. By offering sacrifices on God's altar, the Old Testament believers showed their faith in the Saviour to come. They too were regenerated by the Spirit and justified by faith, but the coming of Jesus and of the Spirit ushered in a new age of power and clarity which overshadowed the age of preparation, not only in the advantages afforded to individual disciples by way of clarity in the truth, but also in the extent of the mission of the Spirit. This was not now confined to one small nation but was to be manifested on a global scale.

It can be argued that the baptism of the Holy Ghost referred to by John is different from regeneration or the baptism of believers into Christ referrred to by Paul in 1 Corinthians 12:13. In the first instance he, Christ, is the baptiser. He is active. He baptises. In the second he is passive. Believers are baptised into him as the head and into his Church which is his body. For we are the Father's workmanship, created in Christ Jesus unto good works (Eph. 2:10). We must not overlook the fact that Pentecost was the work of the Father also, since it was 'the promise of the Father', but due note ought to be made when Scripture emphasises a particular rôle in the Godhead. 'I will send him,' said our Lord (John 16:7). Christ's rôle is active in baptising with the Spirit.

The disciples at Pentecost had been regenerated at an earlier time and showed the marks of the new nature by confessing Christ to be the Son of God (Matt. 16:16,17). They had received the power of the Spirit for the teaching and healing ministry (Luke 9:1-16) and were specially endued with the Holy Spirit before Pentecost when our Lord had breathed upon them (John 20:22).

What then was Pentecost? As already asserted, it was the birthday of the Spirit. But it was also the fulfilment of Joel's prophecy predicting the winding up of the old age and the ushering in of the new (Acts 2:19,20). The speaking in other languages pointed to the fact that all barriers, linguistic and national, were to be broken down, male and female, bond and free, Jew and Gentile—all were now one by faith in Christ Jesus. Unity and blessing (Gen. 12:3) in the anointed Messiah were expressed whereas Babel was an expression of judgment, the human race thereby being fragmented by confusion and disunity.

Christ, being exalted to the right hand of God and having made the promise that he would give the Holy Spirit, then demonstrated his exalted power by that which was seen and heard at Pentecost. This proof of Christ's exaltation and reign at the Father's right hand was not confined to Pentecost. There are six references to Christ being the baptiser with the Holy Spirit, one in each Gospel and Acts 1:5 and 11:16, 'Then remembered I the word of the Lord, how that he said, John indeed baptised with water; but ye shall be baptised with the Holy Ghost.' These words of Peter are of particular significance because the apostles saw in the work of the Spirit at Caesarea the continued result of Christ's reign. Having poured out the Spirit at Jerusalem and at Samaria, which was the first threshold to be crossed from the Jewish to the non-Jewish world, our Lord now poured out his Spirit upon Gentiles who were aliens and strangers to the privileges of Israel. In other words, if these Gentiles are accepted into the fold then the middle wall of partition dividing Jews from Gentiles would be broken down once and for all.

The reception of the Spirit by Cornelius and his household was visible, as it was in the four instances narrated by Luke in Acts, beginning, as our Lord intimated, at Jerusalem, but also at Samaria (Acts 8), Caesarea (Acts 10 and 11), and Ephesus (Acts 19). Ephesus was the centre from which all Asia Minor was evangelised (Acts 19:10). By pouring out his Spirit, our Lord was authenticating the preaching of the Gospel to the ends of the earth. But why did this happen in a visible way in these four instances and not in others? When we say in a visible way we refer particularly to the Holy Spirit 'falling upon' believers (Acts 8:16; 10:44). In falling upon these groups, a visible and audible proof was given of the reception of the Spirit. This visible evidence was, under these circumstances, a necessity. The resurrection and living power of our Lord was proved by the events of Pentecost. The inclusion of the Samaritans, who for centuries had been estranged and separated, was also visibly proved, in this way overcoming a breach or schism which would have proved disastrous to the united testimony of the early Christian Church. Likewise when it came to the inclusion of Gentiles such as the Roman centurion Cornelius and his household, Peter used as his crowning, irrefutable argument the fact that the Gentiles had received the Holy Spirit. This was at the first great Christian Council at Jerusalem (Acts 15). 'And God, which knoweth the hearts, bare them witness, giving them the Holy Ghost, even as he did unto us' (Acts 15:8). Peter's conclusion ought to be well noted, 'and put no difference between us and them, purifying their hearts by faith'. Peter's deductions are clear, 1. The reception of the Holy Spirit proves the inclusion of the Gentiles. 2. The great work of the Holy Spirit is to purify our hearts by faith.

Likewise at Ephesus the Holy Spirit fell upon the group of twelve disciples. Paul's question is a question we could ask any nominal Christian: Believing, did you receive the Holy Ghost? (see footnote 4). The answer to this question by nominal Christians would be similar. We have not heard of the Holy Spirit, or we do not know what you mean when you talk about receiving the Holy Spirit! Ask an evangelical Christian and he answers: 'When I was immersed in water in Christian baptism it demonstrated publicly the reality of my experience of unity with Father, Son and Holy Spirit. It was by the Holy Spirit that I believed in Christ to salvation and by the Holy Spirit that I have persevered in union with the Trinity ever since.' Note how Paul instructed the twelve concerning basic truth. We have only a brief synopsis of this (Acts 19:4). Having taught them, he baptised them which indicates that they had not been Christians before Paul came. They were living in the inter-testamental period and it is important to remember this in interpreting Acts 19. When Paul laid hands on them the Holy Ghost came upon them, and an audible confirmation of their inclusion by the Spirit in the body of Christ was given.

The obvious question is, Why should we not all enjoy this visible and audible confirmation of our having the Spirit? The answer is that the apostolic testimony was unique and extraordinary, yet even with the apostles we find that outside the four groupings (at Jerusalem, Samaria, Caesarea and Ephesus) this confirmation was not given. At least it is not reported. If this was to be the inviolable pattern for individuals it certainly would have been indicated in Scripture. Nothing of a similar nature is reported for the three thousand converts in Jerusalem, the Ethiopian eunuch, Paul, the households of Lydia and the Philippian gaoler, of Crispus or the Corinthian converts. Moreover, it is an accepted axiom in formulating Christian doctrine that we base our teaching on the clear statements in the epistles rather than on the narratives in Acts which report those events peculiar to a time which was unique inasmuch as it was the time of transition from the Old Covenant to the New.

Chrysostom (345-407) referred to the cessation of the Charismata and Augustine, speaking of the Holy Ghost falling upon them that believed, declared, 'these were signs adapted to the time. For there behoved to be that betokening of the Holy Spirit in all tongues, to show that the Gospel of God was to run through all tongues over the whole earth. That thing was done for a betokening and it passed away.'

The signs have passed away because that which was indicated by the signs, namely the inclusion of all Gentile nations in the Church, is no longer under dispute. But has the power passed away? Our Lord said that all power was given to him in heaven and in the earth and on that basis of confidence the world was to be evangelised by us to the end of the age. Did our Lord exercise that power only in the apostolic times or does he baptise in the overwhelming sense now with fire and the Holy Ghost? And what does he mean by fire?

Dunn in his book on the Holy Spirit takes baptism with fire to point to purification (p. 13). But surely a definition of what it is to be baptised with fire cannot be confined to purification? 'You shall receive power' [not purification], said our Lord, 'after that the Holy Ghost is come upon you.' The concept of fire and of fiery tongues rests more naturally with the idea of power than with purification. In commenting upon Matthew 3:11, Hendriksen, in speaking of the baptism with fire, describes power at Pentecost as an 'unprecedented illumination' and, 'wills strengthened, like never before with contagious animation' (Acts 4:13,19,20,33). Surely the tongues of fire resting upon each disciple indicated tongues loosed to fulfil the saying of Joel, 'your sons and your daughters shall prophesy'. A fiery eloquence followed which was seen in Peter's preaching. Unquenchable zeal and holy boldness were in evidence.

We should remember that the unmatched power of God to convert souls lies not in miracles but comes through preaching. There is no reason for the unique signs which attested the uniqueness of Pentecost to be repeated, but there is every reason to expect the same power then manifested through preaching to be repeated over and over again to the end of time. Think of John Livingstone preaching at Kirk of Shotts in 1630 when 500 were converted. Think of the Great Awakening the following century and the preaching of George Whitefield and others. Think too of the revivals of the last century when tens of thousands were turned to God. The fire and the power came down from heaven and will surely come again whenever the Lord, who has all power, wills it.

Is it not right and profitable to use the expression 'baptism of the Spirit' with reference to individuals? Someone may well point out that I have drawn attention to rich meaning of the word 'baptism'. Could there be a better experience than for an individual to be baptised with the Holy Ghost and with fire? If the expression was used to describe experience of the same kind as that in the book of Acts and we had thousands added to the church nothing but agreement and thankfulness could result. But when the term is used to describe subjective experiences which may be self-induced and which do not resemble the glory and power of the thing signified, it is better to use the expression to describe Holy Spirit revivals.

It may be significant that the expression is never used of individuals in the New Testament. It is applied to the four groups only from the one hundred and twenty in the upper room to the twelve at Ephesus in which the Holy Spirit fell upon all inclusively and unconditionally, *i.e.* the Holy Spirit came in a sovereign way not dependent upon special prior conditions being met. Hence my heading, 'baptising the Church'. 'But Christ,' said John, 'will baptise you with the Holy Ghost and with fire?' This was a reference to the first revival and to other awakenings which follow such as that at Caesarea. My conclusion, therefore, is that the baptism of the Spirit has to do with the Church and with revival.

The Church at this time may be extricating herself from the theological confusion inherited from the nineteenth century. The recovery now of a biblical, practical theology of revival could be of great significance and should be pursued.

Our Lord was anointed with the Spirit in a unique way at the time of his water baptism in which he identified himself with all those sinners he was to save throughout history. Having vicariously suffered in their place in a baptism of agony, his atonement has received the approval of the Father who now sends forth the Spirit to unite the redeemed to his Son. To our Lord all power has been given. He has only to ask for the heathen for his inheritance and the uttermost parts of the earth for his possession (Ps. 2:8). The whole earth is destined to be filled with a knowledge of him as the waters cover the sea (Isa. 11:9). How will this be? The answer is that he will reign in the application of his finished work until his enemies become his footstool (Ps. 110:1; Heb. 10:12-17). How will he carry on his work of applying redemption? The answer is that the Father will send forth the rod of his strength out of Zion, that is, a divine energy into the Church and from the Church out into the world. Christ the deliverer will come to Zion. He will turn ungodliness away from Jacob (Rom. 11).

At Pentecost the Father and the Son began to send forth the Holy Spirit and in every subsequent spiritual awaking or revival the Spirit has come in power.   As far as writers are concerned, Jonathan Edwards has probably more help to give than any other on the theology of revival.

Let us look to our Lord, and pray that he will send another great awakening.   If he does, we can be sure that the main result will be the preaching of the Gospel with great clarity, power and conviction to the saving of multitudes of sinners.

NOTES

[1] Alexander Carson devotes 168 pages to this subject in his book, *Baptism, its mode and subjects*.   See also, *The meaning and use of Baptizein philologically and historically investigated*, by T. J. Conant, 1860.

[2] C. W. Parnell (*Understanding tongues speaking*, Lakeland, 121 pages), gets into a muddle because of the Greek preposition *en* (in) which is used in all seven New Testament references; Matthew 3:11; Mark 1:8; Luke 3:16; John 1:33; Acts 1:5; Acts 11:16 and 1 Corinthians 12:13.   Baptised *in* the Holy Spirit.   'The Holy Spirit is never the baptiser,' says Parnell.   This statement is very confusing and unhelpful because it would convey the idea that since we are baptised *in* the Spirit, we cannot be baptised *by* or *with* the Spirit.   Christ certainly is the baptiser.   He sends the Spirit *in* whom and *by* whom we are baptised.   The Spirit is exceedingly active as the outward visible symbols of Pentecost indicate; wind, fire and languages.   And what was the Spirit doing if he did not come actively upon Christ at his baptism, not with fire but in the form of a dove?   In regeneration (1 Cor. 12:13), the Holy Ghost comes like the wind of creation to do a mighty thing to baptise us into union with Christ.   The Spirit *is* the immediate agent in Spirit baptism!   The preposition '*en*' is used of time and place in the New Testament and is connected with agency, i.e. '*with* (*en*) a rod' 1 Cor. 4:21, cf. Arndt and Gingrich.   The *en* must be governed by, and be interpreted within a contextual and doctrinal framework.   The servant in his room is ruled by the master in his palace, not the master by the servant.   Hence it is quite in order to speak of baptism by or with the Holy Spirit.

[3] Some deny that the seal spoken of in 2 Timothy 2:19 is the same as that in Ephesians 1:13, saying that the seal of 2 Timothy 2:19 refers to God's covenant designs.   Nevertheless, it cannot be denied that God's covenant designs eventuate in the elect receiving the sealing of the Spirit as a consequence of regeneration and thereafter bearing the image of Christ in their persons.

[4] Believing ye were sealed.'   We have here an aorist participle with an aorist verb. An aorist participle sometimes expresses antecedent action but not in every case. The context indicates when we should take the two verbs as the two sides of one event: it was when they believed that God sealed them with the Spirit, as in Galatians 3:2, 'received ye the Spirit by the works of the law or by the hearing with faith?' The step of faith is met by the gift of the Spirit. See Dunn, p. 159, and for Greek construction Burton, *Moods and Tenses*, p. 61.

An example of this is Luke's use of the aorist participle with the aorist verb denoting coincidental 'believing received ye the Holy Spirit?' (Acts 19:2).

[5] In 2 Corinthians 1:22,23, 'the establishing' is in the present tense, and the anointing, sealing and giving of the earnest in the past tense.

Three aorist participles are used.   It could be argued that if my thesis is right then the perfect tense would have been used as the perfect tense points to continuing effects of a past action.   My reply to that is that, as in Romans 6:3 and 4, the apostle places the emphasis on the *finished work of God* as the basis of *all* our experience.

[6] Goodwin, *Works*, Vol. 1, p. 248.

Books referred to

From an all-round point of view, John Owen (*Works*, Vol. 3) and Thomas Goodwin (*Works*, Vol. 6) still provide the most useful, comprehensive teaching on the person and work of the Holy Spirit. William E. Biederwolf's *A Help to the Study of the Holy Spirit* is the finest of the small volumes. A criticism that can apply to most books on this subject by a variety of authors including such authors as Stott, Hoekema, Chantry, Kuiper, Bruner, Dunn and Parnell is that while they are most painstakingly careful and informative they lack vitality and power. We are much indebted to these writers for the thinking and analysis that they have brought to the subject to the advantage of us all but surely a book on the Holy Spirit should inspire readers with enthusiasm and impart a consuming passion to labour on in the evangelisation of all the world! George Smeaton's book on the Spirit is wonderfully positive and Buchanan has a whole chapter on revivals. Winslow and C. R. Vaughan are warm-hearted and experimental but Winslow is poor on exegesis while Vaughan, though useful, is by no means a robust theologian. Bruner, while giving an invaluable history of the Pentecostal movement and also providing an excellent overview of the four central passages in Acts, nevertheless speaks like a Roman Catholic Sacramentalist (see p. 263). Dunn is careful and scholarly as to details but reveals no theology of revival as we would expect from a liberal.

Chapter 16

The Enjoyment of Christ

THE enjoyment of God should ever be man's chief aim. This enjoyment is not at the expense of God's glory. Man's chief end is to glorify God, and to enjoy him for ever. The glory of God's holiness and justice is vindicated by the condemnation and punishment of sin in the person of Christ on behalf of believers. By faith in the atoning death we are joined to Christ. Our union with him is a present union with him in his life so that the life we now live is one of holiness and righteousness, and this glorifies God.

So close and intimate is our union with Christ that it is likened to marriage. God ordained marriage for several reasons. Outstanding among these are happiness, enjoyment and comfort. These blessings are never to be severed from the responsibilities of mutual care, faithfulness, support, sacrifice and encouragement.

Believers are married to Christ (Jer. 3:14) and the enjoyment of that marriage is nowhere more clearly depicted than in the Song of Solomon. Warrant for interpreting that book in allegorical fashion is found in Scripture itself. The marriage of the King is described in Psalm 45. Both he and his bride are portrayed in detail similar to that of the Song of Solomon. Who is this King in Psalm 45? Verse six leaves us in no doubt. He is King Jesus. 'Thy throne, O God, is for ever and ever: the sceptre of thy kingdom is a right sceptre.' Hebrews 1:8 quotes this verbatim to describe the king of glory. And who is the bride whose beauty the king greatly desires? She is the Church, for no other is made all glorious within. None other bears a bridal relationship to Christ. The angels do not form the bride. They admire the marriage. It is the joy of the angels to serve at the wedding.

We must reckon too, with the fact that Isaiah has a similar approach in the way he describes the Church (Isa. 54). Also, many of his references are of the same kind (60:8; 61:3; 62:6,7).

The arguments against the allegorical interpretation of the Song of Solomon I find wholly unconvincing.

The believer's enjoyment of his relationship with the Father by adoption is different from the enjoyment of the indwelling presence of the Holy Spirit. The Spirit seals, enlightens, comforts and guides and it is a joy to be the subject of his work. The Christian's enjoyment of Christ differs from his enjoyment of the Father and of the Spirit. The Song helps us to understand our relationship to the head of the Church and I would suggest the different experiences of our enjoyment of Christ as follows:

1. The enjoyment of Christ's unchanging love.
2. The enjoyment of the glory of Christ's person.
3. The enjoyment of Christ's esteem.
4. The enjoyment of communion with Christ.

1. The enjoyment of Christ's unchanging love

This must surely precede all other considerations for it lies at the foundation of our salvation and our relationship with Christ. From eternity he has loved his people with a distinguishing love. He has loved them as the gift of his Father to him. He views them as the reward of his passion and suffering. This love of Christ took him through the overflowing floods of opposition from the ungodly who encompassed him. This love caused him to persevere through the fires of furious justice that lighted upon him and burned him quite up so that he cried 'I thirst', and 'My God, my God, why hast thou forsaken me?' This love of Christ is a love that perseveres, a love that follows the fugitive sinner over plain and mountain, through the thick undergrowth of iniquity, that tracks him down in the dense jungle of sin and rebellion and having surrounded the guilty one cries to him 'Saul, Saul, why persecutest thou me?' It is a love which can and does sweep 'regeneratingly' through a heart. And once it has secured its object are we to think that this love will ever let that object go? The apostle says of Christ, 'Having loved his own which were in the world, he loved them to the end.' Having loved them to the end of Calvary's road are we to think that he will now forego the travail of his soul? Who shall separate us now from the love of Christ?   Shall tribulation, distress, persecution, famine, nakedness, peril or sword?   Should these come upon us we must know that not one of these, nor all of them together, can alter Christ's loving hold upon us.   The love Christ has towards us does not change and even if all of these fearsome trials come upon us we can be assured of his love, and in our experience be sustained and comforted by it.

Two descriptions in Scripture of this love seem to tower above the others.   One is where Paul prays that we might be filled with all the fulness of God (Eph. 3:16-19).   The other is the prayer of the believer in Song 8:6,7.

If we weigh up Paul's prayer (Eph. 3:16-19) we see that his ultimate objective is that Christians be filled with all the fulness of God.   This is tantamount to being filled with all the communicable attributes of God.   It is to be conformed to Christ (Rom. 8:29). The Church is his body.   Christ fills his body, the Church, with his own fulness (Eph. 1:23).   This means that every personality in the Church is different but each one in his own sphere and character is conformed to be like Christ in patience, truth, humility, zeal, love and other virtues.

How may believers be so filled and moulded that in all characteristics they are pleasing to God?   The 'thats' which appear in our Authorised Version help us follow Paul's reasoning:

1. *that* we might be strengthened with might by his Spirit in the inner man, so
2. *that* Christ may dwell in our hearts by faith
3. *that* we, being rooted and grounded in love, may be able to comprehend with all saints what is the breadth, and length, and depth, and height; and to know the love of Christ which passeth knowledge
4. *that* we might be filled with all the fulness of God.

One step leads to another.   We need to be strengthened to know Christ's love, and experiencing that love is the best way to conformity to Christ in being filled with all God's fulness.   The prominence given here to a knowledge of the love of Christ is remarkable.   It is a knowledge staggering in its dimensions.   It is a knowledge in which we need to be rooted like a great oak is rooted in the ground.   It is a knowledge in which we need to be immovably grounded and established.   Ultimately Christ's love is so amazing that while knowing much of it we could never possibly encompass it.

Christ's love is a love to enjoy and what better than to enjoy it as we meditate upon its character as described in the Song? So precious is this love that we want to be certain that it applies to us. Using the words of the writer we make this prayer our own: 'Set me as a seal upon thine heart, as a seal upon thine arm' (8:6). The love with which he loves his people and with which we want to be sealed is strong, intense and of infinite worth.

It is a love as strong as death. Elijah and Enoch were permitted to escape, but apart from them, who has been strong enough to beat back the power of death? Death is inexorable and relentless. Armies fall before death, nations are consumed by it, civilisations are buried under it. Only Christ's love is stronger, for it is a love that has led him to conquer death. As he raises us all from the dead we will be able to sing a song of triumph over death and say to it – 'O death, Christ is your plague, O grave, Christ is your destruction! Death you took me down, grave you consumed me, but Christ has conquered you both!'

His love is not lukewarm nor half-hearted. It is a love like coals of fire which have a most vehement flame. Many waters could not quench his love and floods could not put it out. All the oceans of the world could not drown Christ's love (8:7). If a man would give all the substance of his house for love, it would be scorned utterly!

If someone came to Christ and offered him all the kingdoms of this world for his people, that offer or bribe would be scorned out of sight. Satan did try to lead our redeemer away from his course of purchasing his people and was reproved in no uncertain terms (Matt. 4:8-10; 16:23). Once in the heart of believers, the love of Christ becomes very powerful. It has taken Christian martyrs through trials, tortures and the flames of death. If you had offered Paul all the riches, glory and honour of this world to renounce Christ, the offer would have been rejected with the utmost scorn. 'I count all that but dung,' he said, 'I have renounced all things that I might win Christ and have his righteousness and not my own self-righteousness' (Phil. 3:8,9).

2. *The enjoyment of the glory of Christ's person*

When Mary broke open the alabaster box of precious ointment, the fragrance of that perfume filled the whole house. The presence of Christ is like that perfume. His very garments smell of myrrh and aloes and cassia (Ps. 45:8). It is fitting that at the commencement of the Song these terms should be mentioned. 'Your anointing oils are fragrant, your name is oil poured out.' There is great enjoyment and refreshment of soul in beholding the glory of Christ. Christ's presence is exhilarating to the weary soul as was the ointment poured out to the bodies and souls of tired travellers after a long journey. John declares that 'we beheld his glory, the glory as of the only begotten of the Father, full of grace and truth'. The glory of the next world is this, that we shall see his face and that the Lamb is the light of the new Jerusalem (Rev. 21:23,22:4).

In the Song he is described as the rose of Sharon, the lily of the valleys, the altogether lovely one and chiefest among ten thousand. The word for chiefest is unusual and means standard bearer. Christ is unique. In his person is the perfect harmony and unity of the divine and human nature.

The outstanding description devoted to Christ's person is given in chapter 5:10-16. In answer to the question posed by the daughters of Jerusalem (who can be likened to the enquirers and seekers after truth who attend the churches), the bride asserts that Christ is the chiefest among ten thousand and supports this with eleven descriptions of his person. These are given in the form of striking similes. His complexion, head, hair, eyes, cheeks, hands, body, legs, countenance and mouth are described.

At first the bold, almost stark forms of likeness are daunting to the reader and much more so to the expositor. However, the more study is devoted to these details the more helpful and edifying the verses become. James Durham in his exposition of the Song said that 'many in all ages have shunned to adventure upon it; and truly I have looked upon it, as not convenient to be treated upon before all auditories, nor easy by many to be understood, especially because of the height of spiritual expressions and mysterious raptures of divine love, and the sublime and excellent expressions, yet' he continues, 'we are now brought to essay an interpretation of it'. It may be encouraging to others to know that in weekly verse-by-verse exposition of the Song over the past year I found when coming up to the similes of chapter seven that I felt unable to embark on it and was ready to call a halt, but then felt that would be dishonouring to the Holy Spirit.   If helped with profit through six chapters why register a lack of confidence in the Word of the seventh?   Likewise with chapter eight the passage seemed too difficult at first but in the end proved one of the most satisfying.

Our enjoyment of Christ comes by the contemplation of his glory in his person, life and work.   Take one of the metaphors used. 'His legs are as pillars of marble, set upon sockets of fine gold' (5:15). The cogent pictures used present powerfully before us precise qualities.   The objects proposed in the legs of a man are deportment and bearing, but also strength (Ecc. 5:1; Ps. 147:10).

The pillars of marble tell us of strength which is sublime and beautiful.

As the marble columns of Greek architecture upheld the building with perfect proportion and ease so does Christ uphold the universe. The government is upon his shoulder and of the increase of that government there shall be no end (Isa. 9:6,7).   By him all things consist (Col. 1:17).   The columns are set upon bases of gold.   All civil government is the gift of God to this world to restrain evil and promote good.   While civil rule is marred by much injustice through the depravity of men, yet the principle of order itself with its exercise is of inestimable good to mankind.   'By me kings reign and princes decree justice' (Prov. 8:15).   Whatever virtue or bene-faction we may see by way of protection and peace, employment, order, education, travel, medicine and supply of food and fuel – if there be any good let us trace it to its true source, even the fine gold bases of the column.   The divine nature of our Lord upholds all things.

Not only can we enjoy the contemplation of our Lord who has been given all power in heaven and in earth, but we can benefit in our experience by meditating upon his life and death.   His life was one in which the whole weight of the moral law in all the rigour of its demands was fully met.   Set upon bases of fine gold, his divine nature upholding a perfect human nature, he pleased his Father in everything.   'I do always those things that please him' (Jn. 8:29). In order that we might have remission of our sins it pleased the Father to bruise him, and put him to grief (Isa. 53:10).   He bore the whole weight of his people's transgressions.   What columns these to bear such a weight!   What fine gold to support such a load!

3. The enjoyment of Christ's esteem

'*Thou art beautiful, O my love, as Tirzah, comely as Jerusalem, terrible as an army with banners. Turn away thine eyes from me, for they have overcome me*' (S. of S. 6:4,5).

Here Christ declares his esteem for his Church, comparing her with the most beautiful city of Tirzah and with the majesty of Jerusalem. Her spiritual warfare is conducted with a oneness of purpose, like a formidable army, awe-inspring in its disciplined and determined advance. The spiritual beauty of the Church is reflected and as her eyes turn appealingly to him he cries, 'Turn away thine eyes from me, for they are taking me by storm.'

While there is much imperfection to lament in ourselves we must not underestimate, undervalue or despise in any way that good work which God has begun in his people. It is common in some quarters always to degrade the Church, overlooking the fact that there are innumerable believers in whom God has worked over the years, transforming them into choice disciples. The news of divided churches should not take from us the enjoyment and encouragement to be derived from the great majority of churches where the brethren dwell together in unity and where the fragrance of that unity and love is like the precious ointment upon the head, that ran down upon the beard, even Aaron's beard that went down to the skirts of his garments (Ps. 133:2). Christ's admiration of his Church is unequivocal. If we spent more time expressing appreciation of our benefits and of that mighty work of sanctification which is going on constantly and spent less time moaning and grumbling we would not only enjoy our privileges more but be more encouraging to God's people ourselves.

I have compared thee, O my love, to a company of horses in Pharaoh's chariots (S. of S. 1:9). What shall we say of Christ's admiration of the Church's stateliness, strength and carriage? What strength is ours through Christ by whom we can do all things! Will we not enjoy both the grace he supplies and his admiration of his gifts? He ascended up on high, gave gifts to men, even the rebellious. He has made his Church beautiful. Shall we not admire that and enjoy it?

Thy cheeks are comely with rows of jewels, thy neck with chains of gold. We will make thee borders of gold with studs of silver (S. of S. 1:10,11). As a princess much loved by a prince receives with joy those tokens of his love, we should rest in Christ's love and gladly receive his gifts which are pledges of his esteem (Ezek. 16:11-14; Gen. 24:22,23). In this life we have no jewels, but rather the ashes of the hearth and the dust of the broom.   Peter gives us the clue as to the meaning of these precious jewels when he refers to the ornament of a meek and quiet spirit.   The beautiful graces imparted by the Holy Spirit are the jewels given to make his people beautiful.   Indeed, outward beauty, as was the case with Absalom, is just deception.   Apart from the comeliness of a holy and devout life within, outward beauty is empty.

The most difficult section of the Song, and the part which lends itself least to detailed exposition, is chapter 7:1-10.   How are we to apply these similes in the context of the Christian life?   All Scripture is God-breathed and profitable for doctrine, for reproof, for correction, for instruction in righteousness (2 Tim. 3:16).   It is best to take the section as a whole and say that Christ sees his bride, the Church, in her perfection.   *Thou art all fair, my love; there is no spot in thee* (4:7).   The feet, thighs, body, breasts, neck, eyes, nose and hair are all perfect in form.   The proportion of each part to all the others is perfect.   The conclusion to which we come is that perfection of detail and perfection of proportion are to be sought in sanctification.   Prayer, communion, meditation, fellowship, good works, conversation: in all activities and in all graces, we are to seek perfection even as our Father in heaven is perfect (Matt. 5:48).

The enjoyment of the grace of God exemplified in the various members of the Church should have its place in our own experience. We enjoy Christ's esteem of us by cherishing that which he esteems namely that which is true, honest, just, pure, lovely and of good report (Phil. 4:8).

4. *The enjoyment of communion with Christ*

As union with Christ is permanent and therefore constant in its application, so communion ought to be without cessation.   There are times when our communion is broken.   Then we seek renewal, which, after some effort on our part, may be restored (S. of S. 3:1-5). But sometimes (mostly through our own carelessness) we can go through periods of painful and sustained barrenness (S. of S. 5:1-8).

Enjoyment of communion with Christ is experienced in the context of the Church, particularly so during seasons of revival. It is also known at those times when we especially seek Christ in private prayer or communion. This is not to exclude other occasions such as communion during the night watches.

Communion in the context of the worship of the assembly

The gates of Zion are loved by the Lord more than any homes of believers (Ps. 87:2). Family worship is essential (Deut. 6:7) but meetings at home, whatever their form, can never replace the instituted worship of God (Ps. 107:32). Here, above all other places of meeting, the Lord manifests his presence and meets with his people. The assurance of this basic principle is seen in the glory of the Lord filling the tabernacle (Ex. 40:34,35) and in the same shekinah glory filling the temple (2 Chron. 7:1,2).

In the Song, the Church is compared to a garden enclosed like a plot of ground well laid out and walled around, separated from the world for the delight and recreation of the owner (4:12-16). The most fruitful and beautiful trees and shrubs are planted in this garden which is watered by a spring of life. Many varied and excellent spices are to be found in the garden. These represent the delightsome graces of the Spirit. As spices have excellent, reviving, medicinal qualities, so the graces of the Spirit manifested in the children of God provide joy, cheer, spiritual healing and delight.

The wind of change from the north has a bracing, strengthening, healthy and invigorating effect on the garden, while the warm south wind draws out the fragrance of the spices within it in exhilarating fashion. It is the desire of believers to be fruitful that they may be delighted in by Christ, and that he should come into the garden to find pleasure in the pleasantness of the fruits and spices. The energising power of the Holy Spirit is typified by the wind. Believers pray for and desire his ministry (4:16). In this way the Church fulfils her function of being a haven of heaven on earth, a paradise before the time. There is no communion for the individual believer so sweet, so refreshing and so strengthening as that found within the doors of Zion.

Churches vary a great deal in their spiritual condition, as can be seen by reading the letters to the seven churches of Asia. In many churches where the ministry is consistently good, individuals within find some times to be peculiarly refreshing but other times difficult. To most, most of the time, the local church is a tree of life and joy, the place above all others where personal communion with Christ is renewed and strengthened. Occasionally there are seasons of special refreshment in the local church when the presence of Christ is unusually powerful. Such times are described in the Song.

For, lo, the winter is past, the rain is over and gone; The flowers appear on the earth; the time of the singing of birds is come, and the voice of the turtle is heard in our land (2:11,12). Communion simply means to share in common with others. In the reviving of the Church, we share with Christ the warmth of devotion, for the winter is past. We enjoy the cheer of a better season for the rain is over and gone. We glory in the beauty and advance of spiritual graces. The showers appear on the earth. We are refreshed in worship; it is the time of the singing of the birds. We rejoice in fruitfulness; the fig tree puts forth her green figs. We are made glad by the advance of new converts. The vines put forth their tender grapes and give a good fragrance. As the turtle dove gives expression to the congenial blessings of Spring so the Church sounds forth her praise and joy during seasons of spiritual awakening.

Such times are absolutely ideal for rich enjoyment of personal communion with Christ, affording an excellent opportunity for rapid advance and establishment in the spiritual life. Hence his invitation at such times: *Arise, my love, my fair one, and come away. O my dove, that art in the clefts of the rock, in the secret places of the stairs, let me see thy countenance, let me hear thy voice; for sweet is thy voice, and thy countenance is comely* (2:13,14).

What better incentive to partake of communion could we receive than such expressions of encouragement? Enjoyment of communion with Christ during times of spiritual refreshment in the church is the nearest experience to heaven that we are likely to have on earth.

Communion in private

In contrast to the enjoyment of Christ as he appears among his people in the sanctuary of worship, we turn now to the subject of private meditation and communion. This time the invitation comes from the Christian to the Lord, *Come, my beloved, let us go forth into the field; let us lodge in the villages. Let us get up early to the vineyards; let us see if the vine flourish, whether the tender grape appear, and the pomegranates bud forth: there will I give thee my loves* (7:11,12). The picture is one of the fervent believer getting up early in order to enjoy the refreshment of daybreak and the exhilarating freshness and fragrance of the vineyards. Oriental vineyards were noted not only for the value of their vines but for their layout and beauty. The trees included pomegranates and camphire trees with their lovely, dense, soft, yellow-white blossoms (1:14). The enjoyment of Christ's company is sought in retirement away from distractions. The thought again is of communion or sharing the pleasure of the vineyards and the pleasant trees within it.

More protracted times are also sought, not just an hour before a busy schedule full of responsibilities but a few days away in a desert place alone, to stay in quiet villages where scenic beauty and tranquillity will help communion. All kinds of spiritual matters of a profitable nature await to be shared and uppermost of all is the desire to express gratitude and worship for so great a redemption.

It is not boastfulness but rather sincere gratitude and genuine love of heart that causes the bride to say, *the mandrakes give a smell*. The perfume and savouriness of the spring season illustrate the spiritual fruitfulness overflowing in the soul, *at our gates are all manner of pleasant fruits, new and old, which I have laid up for thee, O my beloved*. Not only well-known fruits such as the pomegranate, but lesser-known, rare and valuable fruits are to be enjoyed. Well-known truths never decline in value, but there are new insights and new appreciations to be shared. The enjoyment of Christ alone early in the vineyards and the pleasure of his company away for a few days, if that is possible, those are some of the treasures of the Christian life.

Communion in the night watches

Should the circumstances of life forbid luxuries like a holiday given over to spiritual reflection, and should some find their physical situation to be the extreme opposite of the rural glories of an oriental sunny climate as portrayed in the Song, they should remember that ultimately these are only pictures conveying vital spiritual realities. A Siberian prison camp, a dark cold cell, a bed of sickness, a hospital ward for cases of terminal disease – such adverse conditions cannot banish Christ from the souls of believers. The night of pain may be long, the bed of suffering protracted, but Christ's presence makes the heaviness lighter and the burden less, for he is *as a cluster of camphire in the vineyards of Engedi*. For their perfume and beauty the camphire clusters were greatly valued as were the bundles of myrrh which were placed by women between their breasts. *A bundle of myrrh is my wellbeloved unto me; he shall lie all night betwixt my breasts*

(1:13). The sense conveyed is one of Christ's presence. He is present through the long night watches with his enablement and comfort to refresh the soul. Communion can consist of sharing subjects, sometimes complex subjects, with the Lord. But communion can also be just resting and relaxing in the knowledge that he will never leave us nor forsake us.

Enjoyment of Christ in all situations: in the assembly of the sanctuary, early in the vineyards, away in the villages or in the night-watches – this is all part of the rich legacy of every believer's experience.

1. *The interpretation of the Song*

F. Godet provides an interpretation of the Song in *Classical Evangelical Essays in Old Testament Interpretation*, compiled and edited by Walter C. Kaiser, Jr. This interpretation fails to do justice to allegory found in Scripture itself and misses completely the glory of that love which is illustrated between Christ and his Church. This historical background concerning the relationship between Solomon and the Shulamite maiden (8:7) is made primary and the whole interpretation made by Godet to rest on that. This surely is incidental and not the primary question. The Holy Spirit would have us preoccupied with the purpose and interpretation of the book as it finds its place within the whole context of Scripture. The providential details of how it came to be written are not unimportant but we can only speculate about that and never be certain about it. But we can use the whole Bible to interpret The Song, Psalm 45, Isaiah 54, Ephesians 5:21-33 and Revelation 21:1-3 are particularly relevant.

2. *Commentaries on the Song*

John Gill is most helpful. He divides every text in a clear style using further subdivisions where needed. Where two interpretations seem possible he expounds both in full indicating his preference, with reasons. His hyper-Calvinism does not appear except in the last chapter on 8:8 where he speaks of the 'elect of God un-called'. We should be concerned, he declares, for all such – not, mark well, for the world, but for the 'elect of God un-called'. John 3:16 would then read, 'for God so loved the *elect of God un-called* that he gave his only begotten son etc.'. But we are concerned for our unconverted relatives and friends and for the world. Not knowing who the elect are, we pray for and work toward the conversion of them all. God beseeches all those unreconciled to himself to be reconciled, irrespective of the fact that he knows who will be reconciled (2 Cor. 5:20).

James Durham is next by way of priority. His commentary is not likely to be available to most since the first edition, dated 1669, is very rare. A. Moody-Stuart on the Song is a very useful book being full, satisfying and exegetically sensitive and reliable. The last edition is dated 1860 and it would be good to see this volume in print again. Matthew Henry, as we would expect, is first class. Useful, but less so than Gill, Durham or Moody-Stuart is George Burrowe's commentary on the Song. Although very brief, the exposition by Jamieson, Fausset and Brown is well worth consulting.

Chapter 17

The Testing of Experience

IT is fitting that we should conclude with the subject of evaluation. All teachings, practices and experiences must be subject to Scripture. Even the most heavenly communion with Christ as depicted in the last chapter requires appraisal. The Scriptures demand that we should be subject to self-examination (2 Cor. 13:5). There are a number of tests to which our experiences should be subject.

The test of doctrine

The apostle John warns that false prophets are numerous and that it is very important to test them in doctrine. The doctrine of the person of Christ is peculiarly vulnerable. Those who claim strong experiences often go wrong at this very point. One questions the experiences of Edward Irving because they seemed to result in erroneous teaching on the person of Christ (see also the deviation of Thomas Smail referred to on page 42). Irving showed other doctrinal aberrations of a most serious character (see page 32).

The question must be asked, Does my experience lead into a clearer and stronger apprehension of the great truths of the Bible? If a minister claims to have special experiences we must ask if this results in his being a better expositor and a more diligent teacher of the Word. Is he more competent in his ability to define doctrine clearly? Is he more robust as a gracious, loving, able, powerful defender and propagator of the faith once delivered to the saints?

Has my experience made me a truth-centred Christian who lives 'on every word that comes from the mouth of God' (Matt 4:4, NIV). Nowhere do we find the prophets or apostles saying, 'I will delight myself in my experiences'. Rather Psalm 119 is summed up well by verse sixteen which declares, 'I will delight myself in thy statutes'.

The 'truth-centred' Christian can say with the Psalmist, 'I have rejoiced in the way of thy commandments, as much as in all riches'.

Here a *delight* is proclaimed; the object of that delight stated, *in the way of thy testimonies*; and the degree of it asserted, *as much as in all riches* (Ps. 119:14).

The test of morality

By the moral test is meant keeping all the commandments of God. Is a person better all round in practical Christian living as a result of his experiences?

If a husband comes home and finds there is no supper on the table and the home and children are not cared for, he will not be impressed by a glowing testimony from his wife about her spiritual experiences! The plain practical teaching of 1 Peter 3:1-7 is much more to the point. Likewise a wife will not be impressed if her husband describes to others his wonderful experiences, but spends far too much time running to meetings, neglects her and the children and has a reputation with his employers and fellow workers for talking too much and not pulling his weight.

We see then that there is the practical test. 'Pure religion and undefiled before God and the Father is this, to visit the fatherless and widows in their affliction, and to keep himself unspotted from the world' (James 1:27).

Let me ask myself the question, Does my experience make me more fervent in visiting the orphans and widows in their need? If my experience is truly of Christ will it not lead to actions of mercy and compassion which have his highest approval?

The test of unity

Our Lord's new commandment to love one another (John 13:34) is heavily reinforced by John in his first epistle. Love for the brethren provides an excellent test for experience. Whatever experience I have had, does it, and has it, contributed toward love and unity in my local church? Have some of the believers been alienated by the narration of my experiences? Is the church more united after my testimony of experience than before? Is there more love among all the members of the church now than there was before?

The Corinthian church was known for its divisions. In dealing with that problem Paul implies in the thirteenth chapter that all gifts and experiences are useless if they do not pass the test of love.

The test of sanctification

God's determined will for his people is their sanctification (1 Thess. 4:3). All things work to fulfil this his purpose, to conform his people to the likeness of his son (Rom. 8:29). In the light of this truth is it not right that we should ask whether our experience, of whatever kind it may be, has contributed toward our sanctification. Holiness or sanctification is both negative and positive. We are set apart from the world and must abstain from all evil (1 Thess. 4: 4-7). Every thought must be brought into subjection to holiness. All evil must be excluded. That is the negative aspect. The positive side is that we must be brought more and more into the likeness of Christ.

Those who testify, in particular, to having experiences of power, need to ask whether their experience has helped them advance in sanctification in specific ways such as outlined by Leith Samuel writing in *Christianity Today* (Jan 21, 1977).

1. to overthrow false ideas and ideologies or systems of thought by which men live (2 Cor. 10:3,4).
2. to face difficulties courageously (Phil. 4:13).
3. to endure physical pain bravely (1 Pet. 4:12-14).
4. to believe Christ is with us steadfastly when we *don't* feel his presence with us at all (Heb. 13:5,6).
5. to fit in with other Christians humbly and helpfully, and to support them in their hours of weakness and distress as well as in their daily routine (2 Cor. 1:4-7).
6. to recognize temptations speedily and to resist them firmly (1 Cor. 10:13).
7. to absorb solid teaching gratefully (Col. 2:6-9).
8. to stand up for the truth uncompromisingly and with courtesy (Rom. 1:14-16; 16:25-27).
9. to recognize continually that our natural resources, i.e. what we are by nature and past experience and what we have achieved by grace, are utterly inadequate to face today's task, but that Christ's grace is sufficient for us this very day (2 Cor. 3:16; 4-7).
10. to have the ability to find some real delight in our weaknesses, for whenever we are weak, then, and then only, are we strong (2 Cor. 10:9-12).

Do we experience the power of the Holy Spirit to face difficulties courageously and to do all the other things referred to above? Our experience, whatever it is, must stand up to such questions. We must never presume that all spiritual experience necessarily results in good. Most tribulation experiences seem to be used by God to advance the sanctification of believers. Sometimes, however, there can be bitterness or resentment which is not good. Whatever the experiences, let them all be subject to the tests suggested, in order that we may be sure that God is glorified in them and by them.

Subject Index

A

Abraham, 112, 114

Adoption, 97-109, 116, 119, 130, 150, 162; as a church, 105-9; brought by Christ, 99-102; through God's love, 102-5

Affections, 9, 10, 57, 80, 92, 131

Africa(-ns), 18-19; South Africa, 32

Alexander, J. W., 95, 96

Allegory: in Song of Solomon, 161, 165-66, 168, 170-71, 172n

Ames, William, 129

Angels: language of, 33, 34

Anglicans, 40-41; National Evangelical Anglican Conference, 41, 42n

Anointing, 149, 152, 158

Antichrists, 152

Anti-intellectualism, 12

Antinomianism, 119

Apostasy, 117

Apostles, 28-29, 113, 147, 154-56

Apostolic era, 12, 31, 33, 34, 154-57

Apostolic Pentecostals, 29

Archimedes, 95

Arminians: and assurance, 112

Armour of God, 123, 134

Arndt and Gingrich, 159n

Art: modern, 16

Assemblies of God, 32

Assurance of salvation, 110-30; and desertion, 126, 127; faith, 113-14; and Gnosticism, 119-20; and health, 125; and Holy Spirit, 115-17; and hope, 113; and sanctification, 114; and sealing, 150-52; defined, 112-14; denied, 126-27; false, 124; in Epistle to the Hebrews, 117-18; in First John, 118-21; in New Testament, 114-15; in Old Testament, 114

Attributes of God, 68

Augustine, 157

"Authentic" existence, 16

B

Balaam, 72, 117

Baptism of (in) the Spirit, 11, 25, 26, 28, 91, 131, 145-60; and Christ, 154-55, 158; and revival, 157-59; for Jews and Gentiles, 155-56; in the church, 153, 154-59; *in, with,* or *by,* 159n; with reference to individuals, 158

Baptism with fire, 157-58, 159n

Baptist Confession of 1689, 111

Baptized into Christ, 147

Barnard, Rolfe, 59

Barnes, Albert, 147

Baxter, Richard, 88-89, 90

Experience: definition of, 9-10; of notion (of idea), 135; vs. doctrine, 25, 42, 131, 133-35, 174

F

Faith, 56, 74, 89-90, 111, 128-29, 142; and assurance, 111, 113-14, 118; and chastisement, 141; and experience, 133; and feelings, 134; and Holy Spirit, 156; and works, 56, 120, 124, 135; in suffering, 132-35
False assurance, 117-18
Filling of Holy Spirit, 149-53; and gifts, 153
Finney, Charles, 146
Flavel, John, 87
Foreknowledge, 103-4
Forgiveness: in the church, 108
Fox, Lorne, 32
Franklin, Benjamin, 95
Free grace experience, 25-26, 43-54, 59, 66, 98, 125-26

G

Gardiner, George E., 17n, 33, 42n
Garner, Drew and Frances, 50-51
Gentiles: and Holy Spirit, 155-57
Gill, John, 172-73n
Glorification, 104
Gnosticism, 118-20; compared with evolution, 119
Godet, F., 93, 172n
Goodwin, Thomas, 111, 127, 129, 151, 159n, 160
Greek Orthodox Church, 41
Green, Michael, 17
Gromacki, R., 34
Guthrie, William, 110

H

Haarhof, Ken, 31, 33, 35
Habakkuk, 91
Haldane, Robert, 76, 147

Harper, Michael, 17, 41, 42n
Hart, Joseph, 83
Healing, 25, 34, 153
Health, 125
Heidegger, Martin, 16
Hendriksen, William, 157
Henry, Matthew, 173
Hermeneutic, 28
Hodge, A. A., 147
Hoekema, Anthony, 34, 160
Holy Spirit, *passim;* and assurance, 115-17, 119-21; and the church, 169; baptizing the church, 145, 154-59; indwelling, 119-20, 148; in filling, 145, 149-53; in regeneration, 145-49; sealing of, 149-52; sovereignty of, 136
Hope, 113; and assurance, 113, 117-18; and patience, 137
Hospitality, 105-6
Howe, John, 96
Hughes, Philip, 150
Humanistic thought, 15
Humiliation: at conversion, 83, 84
Hyper-Calvinism, 172
Hyper-Orthodoxy, 12

I

Intellect: and faith, 56
Intellectualism, 10, 92, 119
Intellectual vs. experiential, 16
Irving, Edward, 174

J

James, 61, 124
Jamieson, Fausset, and Brown, 173n
Jehovah's Witnesses, 19, 152
Jesus Christ, *passim;* 10, 28, 34-35, 55, 174; and adoption, 99-102; and Gnosticism, 118-20; and law, 82; and regeneration, 145-48; enjoyment by believ-

Scripture Index